"Managers wishing to be successful in bringing about change will enjoy reading this book through twice in one afternoon and then start putting the suggestions and guidance into practice that evening. It is delightfully lean: it contains just the material needed for the purpose and leaves out unnecessary verbiage."

Professor Richard Lamming, Manchester Business School

"Anyone who has to make change happen in an organization will find this book invaluable. Paul Adams and Mike Straw show how to deploy powerful change ideas and techniques in simple, practical, manageable ways with lots of examples and useful summaries – a terrific handbook for delivering change."

Neil Rodgers, former Chief People Officer, Egg plc

"This book is a 'must' for those intent on delivering – and sustaining – true transformational change in their organizations. The real life case studies described in the book provide a compelling demonstration of the effectiveness of their approach, which is explained in clear, concise terms. I highly commend it."

Mike Hughes, Director General, ISBA (The Voice of British Advertisers) and formerly CEO, Guinness GB

"The powerful principles in this book will forever alter how leaders approach change and empower teams to deliver outstanding change by cutting through the noise and focusing on breakthrough results. A must-read!"

Andy Weymann, Medical Director, Smith & Nephew

"In a time where change is exponential, leading change is an essential skill for every modern leader. This book, drawn upon insights gained from real business experience, is a refreshing alternative to existing 'run of the mill' and more academic approaches. It is highlighting, in a very accessible manner, the importance of contextual adaptation and of human centric design. A page turner, full of inspiring examples, practical analogies and down-to-earth advice on how to design and implement change in an effective, more engaging and sustainable manner."

Caroline Vanovermeire, Founder of Effra Consult, former Director Organisational Development – Global Support Functions, Barclays PLC and Principal at Heidrick & Struggles

"Need a primer on engaging your team and managing through change? This volume has what you need. As a practitioner with over 25 years of business experience leading change, I've had the pleasure of working with both Paul and Mike over the last decade plus. These two have seen it all, and now they are sharing their knowledge and experience in an accessible, practical book. Follow their guidance – it works...and enjoy the read along the way."

Elizabeth S. Bolgiano, SVP Human Resources, AMAG Pharmaceuticals, Inc

THE LITTLE BLACK BOOK OF CHANGE

THE 7 FUNDAMENTAL SHIFTS FOR CHANGE MANAGEMENT THAT DELIVERS

Paul Adams and
Mike Straw

CAPSTONE
A Wiley Brand

A catalogue record for this book is available from the Library of Congress.

A catalogue record for this book is available from the British Library.

ISBN 978-1-119-20931-7 (hbk)   ISBN 978-1-119-20934-8 (ebk)
ISBN 978-1-119-20853-2 (ebk)

Cover design: Wiley

Set in 11/13.5pt Rotis Sans Serif Std by Aptara, New Delhi, India
Printed in Great Britain by TJ International Ltd, Padstow, Cornwall, UK

CONTENTS

A NOTE FROM THE AUTHORS

Some individuals never reach the level of success they are capable of or aspire to.

Even good companies can struggle, and even the most talented individuals can fall short of what they could or wish to achieve. We have been fortunate enough to work in leadership positions where we were able to achieve great results, alongside talented fellow leaders and staff. It's time to share some of that experience with others like yourself who aspire to great things.

We have had the chance to work with many fabulous organizations, CEOs and inspiring leaders, we wanted to capture the common principles that make transformation successful. After all, so many organizations see the need for change and understand the urgency, but somewhere between that insight and the actual action needed, there is a gap.

We have worked with each other for many years and experienced many of the case studies we share with you. Our aim is both to help others improve, and to provide a new and broader perspective for those looking to deliver effective and transformational change. This book is committed to true transformation, to enable leaders to predictably and consistently make extraordinary things happen by design, again and again.

We would like to thank all those who were involved in the real-life experiences mentioned in this book, and we hope that when they read the contents it brings back good memories. We also give a big thank you to all the staff at Achieve Breakthrough who have committed to developing the heart of the Breakthrough work. Their commitment has meant we have been recognized again and again as the place to go to unleash the power of people to deliver remarkable performance.

We would also like to mention Achieve Breakthrough's sister organization – Inventing Futures. Inventing Futures provides young people aged 9 to 24 with new ways of thinking and acting, shifting ambition, mindsets and behaviours to enable fulfilling lives. One of the purposes of this book is to support our aim in developing young leaders through providing leadership programmes. You can find out more at www.inventingfutures.org.

INTRODUCTION

Why does it take so long to turn an organization around, only to see people revert right back to pre-existing ways?

Unfortunately, this is an all-too-familiar story, regardless of the type of change being introduced; whether it is a new vision, integrating organizations, transformation and organizational performance, change in ownership structure or internal restructuring. However, it is possible to turn an organization around quickly and to create a new future – one where people think and behave differently and deliver extraordinary results together.

Who should read this?

- This book is written for those who wish to deliver change effectively. Whether you are an aspiring senior executive, a middle manager, board director or chairman; it provides a practical, insightful guide to understanding your organization and inventing something extraordinary.
- It is not about "run of the mill" change programmes. It is about delivering extraordinary results – *something that is not at all predictable if results are purely based on past experience.*

- We will give you insights into creating significant shifts in the way people think and behave. This guidance can be applied to any area you wish; from improving service levels to cost reduction, innovation or increasing market share. You can also use it for achieving specific objectives, regardless of whether you are a profit or not-for-profit business.
- This book is based on *real* business case studies, and is written with the aim of being grounded and accessible, rather than purely from theoretical models or processes. We have experienced the business examples shared here first hand through 25 years of implementing and facilitating transformational change with both senior executive and middle management teams.

During these 25 years, we have worked with a multitude of different organizations, including Microsoft, Novartis, Roche, AstraZeneca, PepsiCo, Diageo, Smith and Nephew, Marks and Spencer, Unilever, IBM and Heineken, NHS Hospitals, central and local government and private equity-owned companies such as Talaris and Quintiles.

Inventing something extraordinary for your organization

WHY IS DELIVERING EXTRAORDINARY RESULTS SO DIFFICULT?

If you write down all the things you need to do to successfully transform your organization and achieve superior performance, most lists will include:

- Have a clear vision and strategy.
- Restructure.
- Improve processes.
- Empower people.
- Be creative and take risks.

At one level we wouldn't disagree with this, but the real issue is the level of thinking that is required.

> "The real voyage of discovery consists not in seeking new landscapes but in having new eyes."
>
> *Marcel Proust*

It is not about all the activities people do to transform their organizations, it is often our belief that vision, structures, processes and methodologies will in themselves lead to superior performance. However, a recent survey[1] by Boston Consulting Group showed that 75% of transformation efforts fail to deliver on their promise.

"75% of transformation efforts fail to deliver on their promise."

This book addresses the central issue of *why* they fail and what gets in the way of success.

This missing piece of the jigsaw is our ability to fundamentally change the mindsets, attitudes and behaviours of how the organization works – the context that the organization holds.

---

[1] *Source:* Why Transformation Needs a Second Chapter – BCG Oct. 2013.

The power of context

Let us first explain what we mean by context.

Context is the invisible environment in which we live and work, shaped by a variety of different beliefs and behaviours. To illustrate this, let's consider the example of this picture of fishes swimming in a fish tank. What do you see?

People tend to see fish, rocks and some plants, but they rarely notice the water itself. Context is like the water in the aquarium; rarely noticed, yet critical to our existence. If the water is toxic, everything dies!

If one of the fish jumped out of the aquarium, we can only imagine what they might see for the first time ... the water, and the size and shape of their tank. Yet, when you're in the "water", you can feel the frustration, but don't neces-sarily have access to means of changing it. This dynamic is essential to understand because the water determines whether the fish are thriving, or at best surviving.

Consider the last time you joined a new company – the organizational context or culture is evident to you ... but after a while it disappears into the background and becomes "just the way things are done around here".

In organizations, people often comment or complain about "what it's like to work here", or how easy it is (or isn't) to get things done. In doing so, what they are actu-ally describing is the context or environment in which work takes place. Often we spend a lot of time creating new processes in an attempt to make things easier. But have you ever noticed how all our best efforts to make improvements usually fail to actually transform the situation?

Like the water in the fish tank, no matter what those fish do, the water still affects them. To put it another way, no matter how much those fish move around, interact and make decisions, they will still always be affected by the water. Context colours everything in an organization. People often refer to this as the organization's culture.

> "Culture eats strategy for breakfast."
>
> *Peter Drucker*

As this suggests, if the culture isn't right, you won't accomplish your strategy. Context exists at many different levels: global, industry, organizational and individual. It is made up of the collective beliefs and assumptions held at these different levels, and it influences any decisions that are taken.

At a purely individual level, context is a person's frame of reference. It shapes their views, opinions and judgement – usually without them even being aware of it. Like our fish, unaware of the tank they are in, individuals operate in a wider context.

Consider someone who is accustomed to working for a high-tech start-up being asked to work at the local hospital. This person will probably be used to an environment characterized by comfortably taking their own decisions and creating quick solutions to any problems that arise. They may also be unaccustomed to stringent health and safety procedures.

So, faced with a patient who needs their medication urgently, this person is unlikely to consider the chain of authorization and the required routines in order to administer the medication safely, as this is not the environment they have grown up in. They may therefore decide to act on their own initiative, because their "frame of reference" would be guided by their experience working for a high-tech start-up company, coupled of course with their life outside of work. This is not because of any limits in capability but is more a demonstration of the power of the context of the unwritten tenets of a medical environment.

Context is decisive

So what exactly do we mean by "context is decisive"?

Context shapes an individual's perceptions. It is the foundation on which people construct their understanding of the world, and when you alter context you automatically alter their subsequent actions.

A change in an individual's frame of reference leads to different thoughts, actions and behaviours. The wider context determines if these actions and behaviours will be effective. If you wish to change actions and behaviours, a new context may need to be created to enable people to see a new perspective, which can then open up the possibility for transformational change.

Recognizing and understanding both the organizational context and an individual's frame of reference is a critical step in leading and delivering transformational change.

The power of context

The challenge

In the 1990s, a leading alcoholic drinks company had a business problem that prevented growth in international markets. Due to controls by international tax authorities, it was not possible, economically, to provide the company's international customers with the ability to place a single order for a number of products from multiple manufacturing sites around the world. What appeared to be a simple problem had challenged the best people in the company for well over a year with no progress. Customers had to pay more for their supplies and the company's associated internal operating costs were high.

The approach

To seek a solution, business consultants were recruited and internal teams were assembled to find creative ways to develop business processes and computer systems and a way of working that would satisfy tax authorities (Europe and the IRS in the USA) that the appropriate controls were in place to meet their requirements. The company's annual tax payments were significant (multimillions).

The context surrounding this problem was that protecting the company's tax obligations was the highest priority. The internal tax team was highly skilled and experienced in this area. Their expertise would therefore guide and influence the project team's design of a solution, by providing the boundaries and constraints within which consultants and internal teams had to operate. The power of the tax team with their expertise and knowledge was a force field that influenced the company's decisions both directly and indirectly. Just like the water in the fish tank.

The frame of reference everybody worked within was that international tax is a complex area best left to the tax team. In addition, they would manage all communications with the tax authorities to ensure best practice and that compliance was maintained. Project staff were informed of the need to ask the tax team for their authorization for any new process or procedures that had an impact on tax.

The result

Fortunately, a new member of staff joined the company who had not yet been conditioned and influenced by the context and need for tax department authorizations. After understanding the problem he decided to make contact with the IRS in the USA and then discussed the company's problem and asked some related questions. The IRS responded by stating that the policies and procedures had been updated 18 months ago and there was now more freedom in accounting procedures that would make it easier to provide their international customers with the required improvements in ordering and supply.

The rest is history. A solution for customers was introduced. However, only after spending millions on a project to develop and introduce the most advanced systems and accounting solutions in order to solve a problem that was not there.

The "context" had been guiding the company's approach to decisions. The context was decisive. The related frame of reference had led to assumptions that were out of date. Ask yourself: How often does our frame of reference lead to powerful and poor assumptions? How often do we assume that those with "expertise" know the right direction to take?

If the new member of staff had not joined, millions would have been invested to find a suitable solution that aligned with the context and frame of reference of the internal staff. In short, you must seek to understand the context, and the associated frame of reference, then continuously test the underlying assumptions.

If you have the ability to shift the context for yourself and for your organization, then you will be able to develop the ability to consistently and predictably deliver extraordinary results for your organization. This is the missing piece of the jigsaw.

Until you can see the underlying assumptions, your ability to consistently change the context is compromised. Like an alcoholic who is in denial and cannot break free from drink, the context uses you until you can break free. *It* uses *you*, rather than *you* being able to influence it and create a new context.

> "Until you can see the underlying assumptions, your ability to consistently change the context is compromised."

Summary

WHAT IS CONTEXT, AND WHY IS IT SO IMPORTANT?

- Context is the foundation on which people construct their understanding of the world.
- To transform an organization, you need to alter the underlying assumptions and invisible premises on which its decisions and actions are based. This is altering the sum of the conclusions that people have reached.
- Context determines everything, no matter how good you are.

- Context shapes perception, and when you alter context, action automatically changes too.
- To deliver extraordinary results, you have to be able to see the limitations of what people can possibly achieve and develop the ability to shift personal context, both for yourself and for the people in your organization.
- Actions and behaviours of people follow the context and frame of reference we hold as individuals and as an organization. The context and frame of reference must shift to influence and create motivation for transformational change.

Key takeaway practices

A key practice for you now is to uncover your own and your organization's existing context. To help you to do this, reflect on the following questions:

- What are your people's views and opinions?
- How achievable is the strategy?
- What contribution can each individual make?
- What gets in the way of them being at their most extraordinary?
- What frustrations and challenges do they see?
- Do they feel they can make change happen easily in the organization?

Be very specific and look beyond the initial "responses"; explore these conversations so that you really understand the frame of reference people are holding.

The answers to these questions will start to uncover the sets of assumptions and beliefs people hold about the organization – this is the context. This will either help or hinder your progress.

"The Magnificent Seven"

These are seven context shifts that if you become masterful at managing, will enable you to predictably and consistently produce extraordinary results.

The rest of this book guides you through how to deliberately alter the context for yourself and your organization, introducing and illustrating the seven fundamental shifts that are required. We call these the Magnificent Seven:

SHIFT 1 Letting go of the past
SHIFT 2 Developing breakthrough ambition
SHIFT 3 Creating a bold new vision of the future
SHIFT 4 Engaging the players in the bold new future
SHIFT 5 Cutting through the DNA
SHIFT 6 Keeping the organization future-focused
SHIFT 7 Gaining energy from setbacks

Shift 1

LETTING GO OF THE PAST

In the book *The Merlin Factor*, Charles E. Smith warned that one of the greatest obstacles to performance breakthroughs in organizations was peoples' beliefs. These beliefs are "logical" (to them) and self-limiting about what's possible for them to achieve – and they're purely based on the past.

Lead from the future

Basing today's actions on past experiences seems to make sense; after all, your decisions in the past enabled you to succeed this far. However, using your past as a point of reference binds you to only those possibilities that lie inside the boundaries of that which you know. We refer to this as the gravity of history.

> "Using your past as a point of reference binds you to only those possibilities that lie inside the boundaries of that which you know."

There is an alternative. Instead of leading from the past, you can lead from the future. In order to lead from the future, you need to define a future achievement that would normally be considered impossible at the time of commitment given the existing ways of working, historical performance and current evidence – and then you make an absolute commitment to it. If you look at all the major innovations and breakthroughs in the world, the common element is that they did not seem possible at the time they were conceived. For example, when Mark Zuckerberg created Facebook he thought 1 million users or being a $1billion market capitalized company would be cool. This goal was definitely not possible in most people's reality or Mark's at that time. Now they have just reached 1 billion users!

> "While theoretically and technically television may be feasible, commercially and financially, I consider it an impossibility."
> *Lee de Forest (inventor of vacuum tube/electronic valve), 1926.*

These and similar breakthroughs required a commitment to a seemingly distant possibility.

An organization that becomes committed to an "impossible" future achievement will produce extraordinary results in the present. This concept is at the heart of delivering something extraordinary in your organization.

Avoid normalizing

In organizations where people typically hold on to the past, leaders face the challenge of normalizing. Human beings crave certainty and so we seek to keep the status quo. We try to ensure that uncertainty is kept at bay through our organizational habits and behaviours. This often shows up when people are:

- Looking for solutions within the existing environment.
- Rationalizing and justifying.
- Going for something bold, only to revert to wherever the previous bar was set.
- Being driven by poor assumptions.
- Carefully managing risk.
- Making excuses and reverting to their old ways.
- Finding it hard to resolve problems/setbacks.

"IT'S ALWAYS LIKE THIS; IT HAPPENS EVERY YEAR"

An everyday example of normalizing: consider a typical case of someone making a New Year's resolution to get fit. In January they push themselves to visit the gym at least three times a week, yet by the end of March they are struggling to work out once a week, and the new gym kit has been relegated to the bottom drawer!

The situation has "normalized", i.e. this person has reverted to their old ways.

Normalization occurs when poor situations are allowed to exist, poor service becomes "the norm" and the way things are done becomes accepted. If this is the starting point in an organization, it can present a huge challenge to any change programme.

Recognizing and understanding the normalization paradigm within an organization will help you to generate a new context for change and successfully make any necessary transitions to a new state. Failure to do so can often result in failure to implement change.

How to let go of the past

To enable this shift to occur, it's necessary to adopt new ways of thinking and acting – ones that will enable your people and your organization to pass through the transition. At every stage there is a possible conventional way to *react*, but we have offered some suggestions for ways to *respond* as a transformational leader.

Traditional Leaders:	Transformational Leaders:
• Being self-assured and complacent.	• Listening and adapting.
• Believing their own version of events.	• Progressing and thriving on challenge.
• Accepting and rationalizing organizational myths.	• Being open to new ways of thinking and challenging viewpoints.
• Justifying actions.	• Resolving setbacks and identifying missing factors.
• Having no sense of urgency.	• Acting with urgency.

Creating a vision "free" of the past

The challenge

This organization's cost base was no longer competitive, and they needed to reduce the cost of goods by a dramatic 50%. The primary way to reduce costs sufficiently was to close the manufacturing sites in Europe and move them to China. Senior management wanted to award the contract to their supplier in China; however, there was a four-year history of poor relations between the European site and the Chinese supplier, with a negative cycle of both parties finding fault and complaining about each other. The situation had come to a point where the Europeans didn't believe anything could change, and so they didn't try to make things change. At peak times, this European manufacturing company employed up to 800 staff. The local board of directors, including the chairman and managing director, was not aligned to this change. Over the previous years, whenever a review of company or manufacturing location arose, their rationale for the status quo was so thorough that decision was either delayed or stopped. Data was presented to provide reasons why not.

Progress was continually hampered, and the decision to relocate kept being postponed. The anticipated risks concerned the quality of goods made in China and claims that the relocation could put 80% of the company's sales revenue at risk (multi £ million).

The perceived risk of poor quality in China was driven by pure assumption. The fact was that the existing site in Europe had experienced several years of poor quality production, and therefore the frame of reference for those at the site was that moving assembly activities to China would be a disaster. They believed that the products were highly sophisticated, and the complex engineering solutions involved a "black art" in the manufacturing process.

The approach

Operational Management aimed for comprehensive analysis to support rational decision making; although there was an initial positive intent to support change, hidden behind this were strong negative emotions. The unions appointed an external consultant to review the business case for change, aimed at confirming their personal opinions – but the business case was financially sound, logical and underpinned by clear actions to manage the risks. An external review was undertaken to assess the capability in China, and this was also positive; in fact, many industries had already successfully moved their technical assembly to China. Once the external validations were shared, listening on both sides improved. The purpose was now clear, and the decision externally validated; it became possible to align opinions around the need to change in order to remain competitive. The direction was clear, the decision to proceed was finally taken, and all assembly was moved to China.

The results

The perceived risks of relocation never materialized. Interestingly, once the decision was taken to close the European site, performance rose to new highs and broke previous manufacturing output records.

The change was very successful. The *missing piece* from the perceptions and opinions in Europe was the fact that the existing, complex supply chain was a real disadvantage. Quality improved overall and costs were reduced. There was also consolidation of the existing disparate manufacturing processes, which led to an annual cost reduction of £8 million.

What this enabled

In this example, the antidote to normalization was a clear vision and purpose backed up by an externally validated decision to relocate manufacturing based on proven facts. A strong vision, unconstrained by past experience and biased opinion, eventually ensured there was clarity of purpose. Making the decision and creating the vision "free" of the past enabled the organization to take markedly different action than if they had operated from their concerns and assumptions. This story exemplifies the power of context and how we need to alter people's frame of reference to allow them to take different actions.

What can we learn from this?

How can challenges like these be overcome quickly?

- Let people vocalize their emotions. Work to uncover and understand the myths and the assumptions being made.
- Get all of the perceived risks out in the open, initially without challenging them.
- Get to the facts quickly and make a bold decision. Both detailed analysis and politics can delay a decision until it no longer seems relevant.
- Be prepared to have difficult decisions validated, and consider using external experts to help support, challenge and drive change.
- Communicate the decision to align management and operations, or the need for change.

- Be prepared to make changes within your management team. Not all the management will align with new ambitions.
- Help people to have "a firm grip" on the future vision, so they can let the past "fall away" – have a clear future vision that is meaningful and can be tangibly measured.

Key takeaway practices

- Uncover myths and assumptions by letting people say what is on their minds – don't react.
- Separate facts and requests from the noise – stories and opinions.
- Focus on the outcome you want versus all the difficulties and what people don't want.

"Argue for your limitations, and sure enough they're yours."
Richard Bach

Shift 2

DEVELOPING BREAKTHROUGH AMBITION

When developing breakthrough ambition, it's important to be bold; to be clear about what you *really* want for your organization and why. Then declare it.

Very often, visions and mission statements are simply not bold enough, nor do they articulate where leaders want to take their organizations. You need to be able to:

- Define what you *really* want, versus what you *think* you can do. Management will only break free and achieve extraordinary results when they are engaged with what they truly want, and when they can see the limits of existing customs and practices.
- Create a compelling reason for change.
- Challenge yourself to be bold in your level of ambition: go beyond predictable and expected outcomes.

Achieve breakthroughs:
go beyond predictable

Consider this example:

Imagine someone lives in an apartment block and you ask them: "Where would you like to live?"

A likely response might be, "At the top of the block, so we have a good view."

Ask them, "Where would you *really* like to live?"

They might then respond with: "Well if I could have anything, I don't want to live in a block of flats. I would rather have a house with a garden."

Ask them: "Where would you *really, really* like to live?"

They might then respond: "Well actually, in a big house by the water."

Then perhaps, given further questioning ...

They might respond: "Actually a big house, by the water in a different country!" The point being that most people do not speak freely about what they want as it is always constrained by the past, but through continued questioning people can get in touch with what they are really committed to.

WHAT IS HAPPENING HERE?

We're seeing the person's "frame of reference" change each time they consider their answer to the question. This is because most people set their ambition based on what they think they can achieve given their past history. So, by definition, their ambition is limited to "the top of a block of flats"! If you want extraordinary results you are committing to a future not constrained by your history. Unfortunately, the budgeting process in most organizations leads you to look at what you did last year and what you think is likely this year and the next. All of this makes sense, but it is limited by history and not necessarily what you really, really, really want!

When we consider what our true ambitions are for the organization, this creates a possibility that is not informed by our past experience. It requires breakthroughs in our thinking to accomplish it. Breakthroughs are called for when there is a gap between our current belief in what is possible and the commitment we are making. A breakthrough commitment is distinct from a pipedream – a pipedream is more of a wish or hope. But a new context is specifically defined for a breakthrough and there is clear commitment and action to achieve it.

Breakthroughs are the significant things that need to happen in order to take your organization beyond predictable results. To achieve them, it is usually necessary to step outside the existing context in order to understand and challenge the stretch in the organization's ambitions.

"Breakthroughs are the significant things that need to happen in order to take your organization beyond predictable results."

Make breakthrough commitments

Breakthrough commitments are where we are committing to a result that is not predictable based on past performance. The moment such a commitment is spoken it creates a gap, by design. It forces us to re-examine our approach to absolutely everything.

A breakthrough commitment cannot be achieved by knowing what we know or doing what we have done before, otherwise the result would be predictable. A breakthrough commitment is very engaging – it gives people a view of what might be possible that goes beyond their current thinking. It sets out what could be possible for them, their organization and the industry.

Let's look at an example. Microsoft made a bold commitment with: "A PC in every home." It might not be considered extraordinary now, but at the time there was a significant gap between this commitment and belief at the time about what was possible. When Bill Gates made the commitment there was no precedent for PCs at home – people were actually opposed to the idea – and to top it all Microsoft were not even making computers.

Given what we are asking of people, it's important to develop people's willingness to be uncomfortable and to strive for a significant result or outcome. Most people commit to what they *think* they can achieve; what their past experience tells them. This leads to predictable results, rather than the breakthroughs you want. If people strive only for safe results this will minimize risk but cap creativity.

> "It's important to develop people's willingness to be uncomfortable."

Declare the breakthrough ambition

Very few transformations occur without someone having a breakthrough ambition first. "A PC in every home." Something magical happens when people publicly state what they are going to do – leaders become more committed to making change happen and lead inspirationally.

Unfortunately, a common challenge in making this shift is low levels of ambition in others. Typically this shows up when people:

- Are unwilling to commit, for whatever reasons.
- Are afraid of not being successful and of being vulnerable.
- Rely on past experience to shape their frame of reference.
- Are content with continuous marginal improvement; an incremental philosophy.
- Are more focused on protecting what they have today.

How to develop breakthrough ambition

You can support this phase by adopting the following behaviours:

From Leaders:	To Leaders:
• Comfortable with the status quo or incremental improvement. • Playing it safe with predictable targets. • Reassuring themselves and the organization that existing levels of performance are satisfactory.	• Striving for a breakthrough result. • Going for what they really, really want. • Seeking to define and articulate new levels of performance and rewards. • Creating an environment for people to grow and develop.

Challenging conventional assumptions

An Internet-based credit card company was converting approximately 40% of website visitors (potential customers) into new business. Although management was always looking for ways to improve, the situation had been the same for two years with no real increase in the conversion rate. So what did senior management really want? They wanted a conversion rate of 95–100% for new business. Clearly, based on their history of working on the conversion rate for two years in an effort to raise it beyond 40%, 100% would be "pie in the sky"!

The challenge

What stood in the way of this mission to achieve 100%? There were industry trends guiding them to believe that a 40% conversion rate was acceptable. Therefore, ambition to improve on this was very low.

It became apparent there were some conventional assumptions standing in the way of a "breakthrough":

- If people own a credit card, why would they need another?
- One way could be to take on other people's debt, but credit card organizations don't buy debt on people's cards.
- We've tried everything, so it must be impossible!

The approach

There was a concerted effort with senior management to get them to be present to the thinking and acting that was getting in the way. In acknowledging past conventions, they were then able to consider possibilities that would have previously been disregarded. This shift in awareness allowed them to authentically commit to what they really wanted and in turn challenge all the limiting conventional wisdom within the company and in the industry. This was central to being able to get a breakthrough in the number of people who wanted a credit card who went on the website.

The results

Conventional thinking was challenged, and action changed dramatically.

They became the first credit card organization to offer interest-free balance transfers, smashing existing assumptions and achieving a breakthrough result of almost 100% conversion to new business via their website. They went for a "breakthrough" and became the pioneers of a new market trend for 0% balance transfer! There was now no need to measure conversion rate and zero balance transfers became a game changer for the industry, as recognized by the company's market capitalization at sale.

What enabled this extraordinary result?

- There was an acceptance from the team that "more of the same" would not be enough.
- There was a willingness to be courageous and to "step outside the comfort zone".

- The risks taken in this example were phenomenal, which pushed the ambitions beyond "predictable".
- The actions that resulted from the new ambition of 100% were dramatically different from those involved in increasing website conversion rates to 40%.

This example required creativity and the coming together of many minds to find the breakthrough solution – this is the heart of real innovation and creativity.

Key takeaway practices

- Identify what you really, really want – what would be a breakthrough for you. Distinguish between pipedreams (not believable) and what is predictable, and the breakthrough will be somewhere in between.
- Develop a powerful narrative of why you and others should believe and be excited by the possibility – this is getting yourself on board.
- Declare the breakthrough publically – this has a tremendous effect – no going back now!

Shift 3

CREATING A BOLD NEW VISION OF THE FUTURE

This shift is about creating a bold, empowering vision and mission for the organization that is *not constrained* by *past experience*, together with a compelling reason for change.

A vision and a mission?

A vision provides an organization with a clear underlying purpose for its existence, which guides behaviour and action. To refer to a well-known example; John F Kennedy's vision with regard to US space exploration was:

> *"To become the world's leading space-faring nation."*

A mission is a shared goal, which has a clearly defined end-point in the future, and the success of which is measurable. In 1961, John F Kennedy declared the following mission:

> *"I believe that this nation should commit itself to achieving the goal, before this decade is out, of landing a man on the moon and returning him safely to the Earth."*

However, it was how Kennedy engaged people that made the difference – what really stuck with people was how he made them feel when he declared "A man on the moon (at the end of the decade)."

Remember delivery AND content: It's what you say AND the way you say it

A recent survey[1] highlighted a significant communication challenge for leaders:

- 86% of business leaders rate themselves as good or very good communicators.
- Only 17% of their stakeholders agree with them.

In the words of successful, modern-day leader and former US President Bill Clinton:

"You measure the impact of your words, not on the beauty or the emotion of the moment but on whether you change the way people not only think, but the way they feel."

What are you going to say that will inspire your people about your strategy?

How are you going to do it?

What are you intending to leave them thinking and feeling?

Alignment will only be achieved and appropriate action taken when management is engaged in a common purpose

---

[1] *Source:* The Leaders Voice – Clarke and Crossland.

that they recognize will provide a value greater than their perceived loss or risk.

Possibility needs to be constantly created by leaders, it doesn't exist naturally. This enables their people to act consistently with that possibility until it becomes a reality.

Use burning platforms

Burning platforms are pivotal points or situations; an impending crisis where an organization must "do or die". A burning platform can quickly and easily create a common purpose, as illustrated perfectly by the Nokia story. CEO Stephen Elop attempted to rally the troops in 2011 with a brutally honest company-wide memo. Within it he explained the challenges the company faced as a result of their failure to adapt to shifting markets: in short he used language to suggest that Nokia had been slow in responding to the developing smartphone market and that their effectiveness in creating and achieving countermeasures was not good enough. He also cited that the situation was mainly due to a Nokia internal issue and unless they collectively did something different they would no longer exist.

This email to all staff highlighted a critical issue that had put the company on a burning platform. Survival meant jumping off. Change and taking risks were a condition, not an option, for survival. It is a great example of how a leader has tried to alter the reality of their people by changing the context within which they're operating. In this case, it didn't stop the later takeover by Microsoft and potential disappearance of the brand in 2014. However, it was a very powerful memo that has become an example of how leaders can galvanize their organization towards a change. If you want the full email you can Google it.

There are many other ways that one negative aspect of the business can be prioritized for action through either deliberate decision or crisis; such as poor service, lack of sales or poor quality standards. The selected burning platform immediately provides a clear purpose and helps to rationalize the resulting decisions that are inevitably needed.

Avoid the pull of the past

When leaders articulate a new vision or mission, the gravitational pull of historical rituals and people's existing assumptions and beliefs often water down both the original ambition and the genuine desire for change.

A *Harvard Business Review*[2] article talks about the example of a CEO, George Fisher, who failed to get his organization to take a different view of itself.

In 1993, he took over the reins as CEO at Kodak, having left his position as CEO of Motorola. Under his leadership Motorola had thrived, increasing

---

[2] *Source:* Kodak and the Digital Revolution – *Harvard Business Review*, Nov. 2004.

market share and profitability. He was therefore seen as the person to take Kodak to a new level.

Having spent some time in Kodak, it was clear to him that the business needed to diversify and make strong inroads into the digital camera sector. They had some of the best digital technology within the industry, so whilst there were some unknowns, the organization was in a strong position to move forward swiftly.

In sharing his vision of the future with his senior team, Fisher told them that the "film" industry was dying and they needed to move in a different direction. But the senior team was fully committed to the business as it was – "a film making organization". "We don't do digital!"

George Fisher failed to shift the thinking and context of the organization – that "we make film and that's our business".

This is an excellent example of how an organization's bold future can become normalized – and Kodak has now become part of history!

Creating the future

One of the key ingredients in building a bold new future is the ability to communicate this future. This is a very creative art and encompasses painting a vivid picture of a future that taps into the emotions and thinking of different types of people. We are all different, but at the core are the same principles that when combined together can create an inspiring vision of the future.

The following are the key ingredients to mix together:

1. **Resonance with people** – understand their motives and what concerns people and ensure you tap into that. Tune into the way people are currently thinking and feeling and ensure your speaking resonates with how they are listening. Like an old-fashioned radio that crackles until you move the dial and then the pure sound emerges – which is what you are metaphorically doing – you are tuning into how they listen. Once tuned in, your credibility and the picture of the journey you are taking them on can be created. Remember, the more tuned into them you are, the more power your speaking will have!

2. **Words matter** – how and what you say matters. Think of all the great speeches and comments – the choice of words is critical as it can create a reality for people and a mental picture of the future as a result of a change or shift in their world. Words and rhetoric can either be uniting or divisive in change – pay attention to the words used. In an organization we worked in, the senior leader announced to the group that he was no longer the project's sponsor – it was an executive more senior to him. His intention was to show that the initiative was now so embedded that it had sponsorship at a more senior level.

However what people heard was that the senior leader was not committed anymore – the opposite of what he meant – so be careful what your words suggest and build in people's minds.

3. **Memorable** – choose a memorable image, slogan or headline to convey the essence of what you are aiming for – it allows people to hang on to what is being communicated.

4. **Big picture and detail** – it is important to communicate at all levels. The big picture is critical for elements of the future in order to elevate people who are bogged down in their daily routines. The big picture gives people the meaning and context for change – it is the dream and shows what will be different in the future. The details behind the big picture are also important because sometimes people don't understand what the vision is without this detail. They nod at the words, but do not hear the music and get the meaning – as a result, they don't know how to dance to the tune.

5. **The request** – this is often missed. This is the specific, clear and candid request to those being communicated to. The request is simply what action you want people to immediately take following this communication. In our experience this part is often missing from creating a bold new future, so people are left wondering what they are supposed to do differently. Their response is often to go back into the spectator stands at the sports ground and observe what the next action is, when what you want is people to get on the pitch and play!

6. **Continual process** – the communication of a bold new future is continual; you are always looking for opportunities to inform and reinforce the message every week and every day. All communications or conversations are opportunities to drive the message home.

Follow this six-step process continually and you will see the bold new vision come to life and start to be built upon and continually generated.

Understand the power of emotion

A common challenge when creating a bold new future is being able to recognize the power of emotion and handle it in a positive way.

Emotion typically shows up in organizations in the following ways:

- Opinions, stories and emotions drive behaviours/culture.
- Fear of change and vulnerability.
- When decisions are taken these can be perceived as irrational.
- A feeling of being overwhelmed.
- A lack of direction and purpose.
- "Commentators" become a strong force recruiting supporters for their views and opinions.

Commentators are those that sit on the sidelines, providing opinions and views to others. Often they have little evidence to support their claims. The commentator plays a role similar to the "leader of the opposition" in politics. For example, discussing with you what should have happened that didn't. Who should have done what, etc. As you may know, the leader of the opposition is a role where you cannot really lose. They may comment on the challenges against change, identify the risks, and can amplify their opinions to whatever level they wish. Generally the commentator cannot be proven wrong until after the event. These people play a powerful influencing role that can be negative if their assertions and actions are not challenged.

If emotion is not managed, expect commentators in the business to create a rationale so compelling that "righteousness without fact" will prevail. As a result, an overwhelming desire to "do the right thing" often masks the real problems and drowns out the facts. A leader operating within this situation needs to have the organization orientate themselves around the future and mission, to help them compensate for the likely irrational emotional reactions that can drive behaviours.

USE EMOTION AS A CATALYST

Managed in a skilful way, the power of emotion can be used to galvanize change, as seen in the next example.

The power of emotion

In the summer of 2008, a healthcare company received a letter from a UK customer concerning inadequate supply of a specialist skincare bandage, for treating difficult skin-related problems.

The letter, from the mother of a young boy, described her visit to the local chemist to obtain a repeat supply of the product. The pharmacist responded with an "out of stock" apology, estimating additional supplies within three weeks, adding "The factory can't make enough due to manufacturing issues."

In her letter, the mother raised her son's medical condition; a severe skin complaint that was very painful. "Without this product for three weeks it will be unbearable for him. Do you realize the impact of factory issues on the wellbeing of a young boy? He will be up all night. We have little hope of any rest due to the pain. Is there really no way of getting more bandages quickly? Could the company please respond, and let us know what can be done to help? Please ask the factory workers if they realize the impact of their actions."

The challenge

The letter was highly emotional and hand written. It highlighted the direct consequences of the operational problems at the factory. At the time, suppliers were consistently letting the company down, frustrations on site were high, overtime was restricted and every day more challenges arose in reaching agreements between management and staff. It was also around the time of pay negotiations. As a result, authorized overtime and goodwill from staff had been steadily reducing for what seemed to be good reasons.

The approach

Senior management posted the letter on notice boards, and it was a leveller for all concerned. Reading it made managers and factory workers alike feel terrible. The impact was amazing; within hours people got together independent of role, seniority and status and discussed action.

Emotion took over.

The results

Over the coming days and weeks, the respective manufacturing lines performed at levels not experienced before. Within days, raised output led to a rapid replenishment of UK supply chains to chemists and hospitals, and a special supply was sent to the mother for her son.

In this example, the letter gave the organization new insight into a customer's life, and it got into the right hands for something to be done about it quickly.

The way events unfolded was outside the company's normal operations.

After all, the customer service department would usually have handled this type of matter, and it would have been unlikely to galvanize any immediate action. When this type of information is received, how often is it used in a way that unfreezes an organization?

"Without this for 3 weeks it will be unbearable for him.

Do you realize the impact of factory issues on the wellbeing of a young boy?"

The problem was very clear. It translated across the breadth of the organization, illustrating how powerful it can be to create a context for people that is meaningful for them. The rationale for change and also the request for action were crystal clear.

Cultural misalignment and failure to agree were dissolved. What happened was unexpected and extraordinary. Normally people wouldn't even have tried, but their frame of reference had been changed by their awareness of the customer's distress.

If this hadn't happened, it is likely that management would have accepted the situation and continued to try to negotiate more effectively with unions and suppliers – and as a result there would only have been marginal improvement. In creating this exception to the rule, the organization became unfrozen, and something happened that was extraordinary. The organizational culture was reshaped, which meant that new things could happen – the same people in the workforce achieved different results.

To put the situation into perspective, the factory included a staff base of around 1000 people at the time, yet the response time across the whole site was equal to that of a small, well-informed team. No issues or constraints were raised in relation to manufacturing line performance or quality of product (first time pass). No overtime or meal break discussions.

A burning platform was created in a positive context. This was not operational fire-fighting, but galvanizing people for the common good, and it triggered huge positive motivation. The common purpose was so strong that the issue of personal risk was dissolved and any perceived risks, such as the impact on pay negotiations or overtime agreements, were outweighed by the advantages.

The letter had a huge impact on the culture of the company – unknowingly, they had not been staying true to their vision. The customer experience for the mother and son was very different from the company's vision, which was to help save lives and improve quality of life. Although the employees were proud of what they did, they didn't realize that sometimes they weren't actually doing it! The mother's letter embraced the company's raison d'être and motivated everyone to achieve what the company had originally set out to do.

The difference one individual can make can be significant, whether inside or outside the organization. Given meaningful context, individuals have the potential to create a culture shift in the organization. Interestingly enough, it is unlikely that the mother who wrote the letter even realizes the impact of her actions.

WHAT ENABLED THE SHIFTS AND THE SUCCESS?

- Using emotions to align the organization with a clear and meaningful purpose.
- Creating a new context that was meaningful to individuals.
- Surfacing and managing negative emotions.
- Creating unpredictable circumstances for people, leading to the delivery of extraordinary results.

How to create a bold new future

Here is what is needed to make a change:

From Leaders:	To Leaders:
• Speaking their views and acting like "commentators".	• Driving conversations towards desired outcomes.
• Complying with rules and opinions.	• Being active decision makers, breaking the rules as necessary.
• Responding to concerns and complaints.	• Making direct requests based on factual merit.
• Being confrontational.	• Being adaptable.

SURFACE AND HANDLE NEGATIVE EMOTIONS

There is a natural tendency for people to be pessimistic about change, and to fear the worst is going to happen – the fear of loss is greater than the desire for gain. It is useful for leaders to both anticipate and explore this. In fact, there are many cases where, despite negative emotions associated with an office or factory closure, performance has actually exceeded previous norms. This happens primarily because once the historical grip is broken there is a new clarity of purpose. Existing ways of working, which may actually have been holding people and performance back, are less relevant than before.

> "The fear of loss is greater than the desire for gain."

Leaders can be vulnerable when emotions run high, because decisions taken at such times can be perceived as being irrational. Our experience has shown that it is best to avoid confrontation based on rational facts, when negative emotions are running high, because this form of confrontation can quickly erode the power of a leader. It is more effective to work through issues patiently, to acknowledge the emotions and if necessary leave the situation until emotions have simmered down.

> "It is best to avoid confrontation based on rational facts, when negative emotions are running high."

An agreement that follows a period of negotiation can sometimes become a compromise, to which both parties need to align. Whilst alignment may not be the preferred solution for either party, it does move the organization forward on the matter being negotiated. But there is a further risk once the change has been introduced – often, what is implemented is different from that which was expected. In order to prevent the situation normalizing again and to keep success on track, be prepared to re-convene to regain alignment.

Key takeaway practices

- Tune into listening – make a note of the key conversations, concerns and aspirations of people that will be impacted positively by the change.
- Practise creating a story that stirs up people's emotions and interest (gets people to stand up, listen and want to commit freely) communicated in a way that promotes a strong image and provokes emotions in people.
- Ask people after the communication what they heard – this will allow you to assess your effectiveness.
- Practise making powerful requests to the people you are communicating to – ones that get people on the pitch versus in the stands watching!

ENGAGING THE PLAYERS IN THE BOLD NEW FUTURE

To create something extraordinary, you need to redefine what people believe is possible and identify what is missing. By "what is missing" we mean the required shifts in thinking and behaviour, together with the standards of performance that are necessary for the organization to exceed in the industry and market they are operating within.

To create a real transformation you are looking for the limitations of what is possible; the boundaries of thinking. This is where imagination and creativity are required. Look at situations through different lenses in order to break out of predictable existence and therefore predictable results.

"Look at situations through different lenses in order to break out of predictable existence."

There are many pathways toward igniting your people's creativity through their engagement in the vision. We aim to provide you with insights into how you can unlock their imaginations.

Valuable insight and inspiration can be gained from looking outside your frame of reference; for example, at a completely different organization, even in a different line of business.

Consider this interesting example, which involved Great Ormond Street Hospital working with Ferrari.

Looking elsewhere for inspiration

The challenge

In the mid-1990s, the fatality rate of cardiac patients in transit between Great Ormond Street's Operating Room and the Intensive Care Unit became a priority.

Obviously concerned, management took a conscious decision to look outside their existing frame of reference, asking "Who successfully manages complex transitions under high levels of pressure? And who does it really well?"

They decided the answer was Formula 1 pit crews. These high-tech teams specialize in high-speed transitions; managing cars pitting from an incoming speed of 200 mph in an average of just 20 seconds. The World Record is held by Red Bull – for a 2-second pit stop. Ferrari's modal average for errors during pit stop was an amazing zero, meaning they were more likely to make zero mistakes than to make one mistake!

The approach

This amazing track record inspired Great Ormond Street's Head of Operating Theatre to contact Ferrari's Technical Director, who flew to London to observe their procedures in theatre. The Operating Theatre team was then flown to Monza to observe the pit crews in action. In particular, they noticed the pivotal role of the STOP/GO person, who is in charge of making all the vital checks before the car leaves the pit. Not only did they redesign their whole transition process following the report and observations of the F1 crew, they realized there was no one in the operating room performing the STOP/GO role at Great Ormond Street, so they introduced someone and it led to a breakthrough! It is amazing how a fresh perspective can help you see things that others miss: this is the power of going outside the normal frame of reference.

The results

Results were extraordinary, and fatalities during transition dropped dramatically! The technical and information errors per handover fell by over 40%.

In our experience, as illustrated here, the greatest barriers we face to achieving "breakthroughs" lie in the fact that we often live inside our own four walls. So we tend not to look outside our own industry, our organization or even our own department when looking for solutions and inspiration.

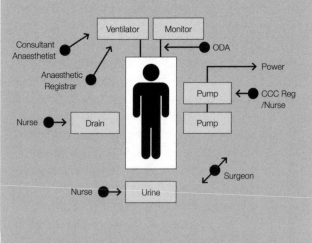

The surgeons called on the mechanics for advice!

Create the new state – and stay there

In most organizations, people are asked to do more things, more quickly and to be more creative with fewer resources than before. In addition they are then monitored for staff satisfaction! This makes it difficult for leaders to motivate people to change. The ability to authentically turn this dynamic around is critical to success. Unless you have leaders and managers with the ability to take people to an empowered state of mind, this challenge can quickly block an organization's potential.

You need to create this empowered state, but also stay long enough in this "new place" to be able to think big and supply sufficient opportunity for both innovative change and extraordinary performance.

People need to be accountable for addressing what is missing if they are to be in a powerful place to lead the implementation of change.

All of us often face the challenge of in-the-box thinking, which typically shows up in the organization with:

- Predictable ways of operating.
- Complacency based on out-dated industry sector knowledge.
- A tendency to maximize predictability and minimize risk.
- Reverting to type.

Recipes for engagement

To improve engagement when a shift or change is required within an organization, we are going to look at control, alignment versus agreement and the need for participation.

Firstly let's discuss control. Many organizations make an assumption that an effective way of unfreezing the organization or mobilizing a change is by getting the person at the top or "board of directors" to make an announcement that "the company is going make this change". Then change managers or department managers spread the word that they have *the endorsement or mandate from a decision at the top.*

Clearly any organizational shift or change needs to be in line with the direction of the company or it is likely to come to a stop quickly. Change will be easier with senior management alignment. However, hiding behind an endorsement from a decision at the top, as described above, can be a blunt instrument when used as the primary reason for change. Potentially, managers use this endorsement to avoid dealing with the key people requirements for change when trying to deliver a vision. The only time this can work is if the organization is small enough in numbers and/or all in a single location or office.

Be aware of how power is exercised within your organization. For example, don't assume the power of the CEO, president or business leader can directly lead to a shift in a company or deliver mobilization or alignment across the organization for a change. At this level of seniority, the power of the role comes from the direction set for the company and gaining and maintaining associated alignment of both internal and external stakeholders.

To put this in perspective, getting the business leader's decision to make a change in a regional office, several layers of management below, with a geographical distance between HQ and the office location, is not going to be effective. It will be out of context and the "message" will get diluted.

Good senior business leaders understand that real power is never needing to use it. Ability to influence is very important. The difference is between having the "authority to influence" rather than "influence through authority".

"Real power is never needing to use it."

Therefore, if you and your team have a vision, think first about:

- Who across the organization will be directly affected by the change? Who needs to know?
- Who are the senior management or teams that need to be engaged and support you?
- More importantly, what are the benefits for others? These benefits must be in context with the world of those involved or affected. It is most effective if the benefits positively impact external customers, i.e. not just your own area.

Benefits of a change need to be clearly defined, be simple and clear. Words, phrases and operating procedures in your workplace are unlikely to be easily understood by others. Companies develop their own language.

"Benefits of a change need to be clearly defined, be simple and clear."

To summarize, let's take the example of a customer service centre wanting to completely change and improve the way external customers are invoiced and pay the company for services or products they have purchased. This change might improve cash flow for the company and raise the efficiency of the customer service department. However, the sales staff might have a significant role in implementing this change and have to deal with the customer reactions (positive or negative). Legal departments might have to change contracts or terms of sale. Manufacturing might be too far away from the change to understand your resulting departmental benefits, so see no reason to get excited. Their engagement and enrolment is likely to be less than it could be.

Yet, if the change is cited as providing an important "point of difference" for the company relative to its competitors, it has a broader context and impact. It could move the company forward in using technology to support and help customers. Sales staff could sell more as a result. Terms of purchase might become more simplified and contractual terms less onerous, helping the role of the legal department. So if customers pay more regularly, repeat orders are likely to be more regular and as a result forecasting for stock will improved. A manufacturer's dream.

These statements above present a positive and more engaging purpose to stakeholders. Now, without mentioning the customer service centre benefits from the change, we have a story to engage others.

The stronger the benefits for stakeholders, the more they are likely to put your change at the top of their action list.

ALIGNMENT VERSUS AGREEMENT

Too often change is hampered by the assumption that agreement from all those involved in the change has to be reached before a shift can effectively happen. Obtaining total agreement on a sensitive, complex matter or issue is very difficult and has a low probability of success. However, alignment can be achieved. Alignment to move forward towards implementation.

It should be noted that achieving alignment can take investment in time. Acknowledgement should not be confused with alignment. In some countries perceived alignment does not lead to a group aligning behind action in a direction or purpose. In the West, if alignment is reached a project or change moves forward. For example, a vote with a majority provides direction. In some Asian countries it can be more challenging, with emotional alignment, procedures, ritual and routines all needing attention.

The most important lesson about alignment is that it does not last for long. Be patient without losing your determination. Teams, departments, will constantly need re-aligning. As discussed in other areas of this book, commentators and those with interest rather than commitment will fill gaps in understanding with ideas, views and opinions that create ambiguity. In the absence of a clear direction they will create momentum in potentially different directions. Don't expect alignment to last and prepare to realign several times. Ambiguity will exist and will be created by others.

PARTICIPATION

For an organizational shift to be successful, however large or small, participation of all staff across the company will have a positive impact and is therefore very important. To achieve this objective, creating an epidemic across the organization with positive emotions and support for the shift really helps. The more engagement from others across the organization, the higher the probability of their participation. The vote for Scottish independence in 2014 provides an excellent example. The power of emotion created by an epidemic supported by public interest (worldwide), personal pride, and a clear deadline with a purpose (a yes or no vote on a defined date).

> "The more engagement from others across the organization, the higher the probability of their participation."

Emotion played a major role in voters' decisions. Commentators helped create emotion and the subsequent epidemic across Scotland that led to so many people taking part in the build up and final voting.

A shift was created that was independent of the resulting "no" vote. Government and political parties participated in trying to guide emotions and stakeholder opinions towards a different outcome than Scotland's independence. As you may know, this was a very difficult task as emotions were running high, and required significant effort to avoid a "yes" vote for independence.

You can create mechanisms within your organization to drive engagement, for example, by creating "pioneering teams" – a significant step above the classic staff suggestion team where you task the lower levels of the organization to drive organizational change or tackle those most hated issues in the company. The aspects of this staff approach that work well are to:

- Have them come up with the ideas and have the organization select the top ones to prioritize.
- Support the successful teams with coaches, mentors and training if needed.
- Create short deadlines, e.g. what could they make happen in just 100 days?

Imagine if the same participation and engagement could be achieved in the shift you need to create. The good news is that a similar situation can be created. If a change has benefits that attach emotional as well as functional or procedural benefits, the power of purpose created will very likely lead to a shift.

"If a change has benefits that attach emotional as well as functional or procedural benefits, the power of purpose created will very likely lead to a shift."

Endorsement from the top helps, but should not be over used. Create a clear purpose, be clear on the benefits and communicate through traditional channels as well as viral ones: coffee machine conversations are powerful. Misalignment will occur. Expect to need to reach alignment more than once. Investment in time will be required. Be prepared to be patient. Don't underestimate the power of emotion ...

How to engage players in the bold new future

In supporting this transformational shift, we are starting to show people the difference between the old practices and the new game. Here, you need to shift your focus and apply specific skills:

"From" Leaders:	"To" Leaders:
• Finding rational and creative ways to justify poor performance. • Accepting assumptions at face value.	• Opening up problems and taking action. • Defining a new context for problems and taking action, defining new expectations for superior performance. • Challenging assumptions and leading by example.

The following example illustrates how predictable ways of working can hamper creativity and dampen aspirations for the business.

Pushing for "out-of-the-box" thinking

After years of marginal growth and a focus on cutting costs to grow profit, the CEO wanted to shift the company towards a higher growth strategy. The company was trying to "save its way to success" – not a good long-term strategy.

The CEO announced: "We're doing the same thing over and over again and then expecting something different."

The challenge

The company aspired to grow sales revenues by double digits. They developed detailed business plans with supporting analysis and advice from consultants. Management was not short of creativity, but they lacked innovation and, therefore, the capability to implement their business plans and get the desired results. Why?

The company had habits that were preventing "out-of-the-box" thinking. The existing ways of working were stronger than the management's commitment to change.

For example:

- Stretch revenue targets were introduced into bonus incentive plans, but the profit was weighted higher than the revenue targets. So if revenue targets failed, bonuses were still possible so long as costs were cut and profits secured.

This was a self-fulfilling prophecy.

- Sales pipelines were developed, and sales opportunities and risks were identified. Commercial teams therefore had the potential to deliver additional revenues and reduce sales risks by solving associated problems. The finance teams worked diligently to challenge the probabilities associated with the opportunities, making provision for the risks materializing. As a result the sales forecasts were lowered, so the probabilities of sales opportunities went down – and the risks were mitigated by cost cuts to protect profit.

This led to routine practices in which every stretch plan was normalized back to "doing as we have always done" – lowering forecasts and cutting costs. No matter how much the company planned for a change in priorities, existing routines continued to thrive on "in-the-box" thinking. Resulting in no revenue growth.

The approach

Honest and sometimes uncomfortable conversations about performance were held at executive management meetings. The thorny issue of constant under-achieving was challenged publicly, and the need to think and behave differently was recognized.

Today, leadership are now working to new targets that positively weight the company's revenue aspirations. Budgets have been rebalanced to enable the required investment in new technology. Incentive plans have been put in place, and constant reminders to keep behaviour in line with incentives and to prevent normalizing behaviour from re-emerging.

The outcome

The company is now delivering results in a very different way. For example, focus on fewer objectives that are more important has helped turn around key areas of the business. Whilst internal targets are not always achieved yet, growth is achieved on a consistent basis and in a very difficult global market and ahead of the majority of competitors.

Key takeaway practices

• Ask people what is missing to fulfil the vision or request – this always leads to people telling you what is required and moves conversations away from what is wrong and lacking to what is missing and can be provided.

• Ask people be accountable for addressing the missing areas they see – avoid taking the responsibility back.

• Seek alignment – following the process of making proposals, ask people if they are aligned and if not what is missing for them; have the discussion.

• Make more requests than promises – powerful engagement comes from others taking the actions and making the proposals happen, not from senior leaders taking the action.

CUTTING THROUGH THE DNA

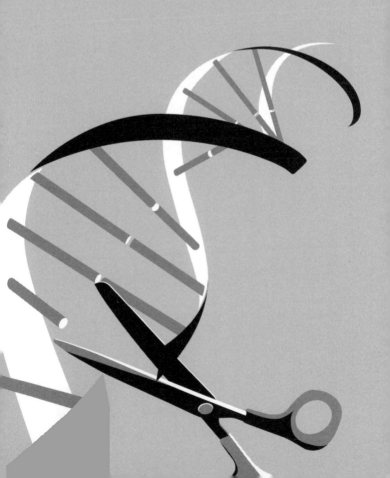

We have already said that context is decisive, and it determines the actions people will take. By definition, the ambitious new future cannot be achieved with people thinking the way they have always thought, and doing the things they have always done. We also know that people tend to revert to their old set of assumptions. So a shift is critical, and can only be achieved by tapping into the organization's "DNA".

Discover the unconscious DNA

When you identify and understand the organization's dynamics, structures, existing rhythms and assumptions, you know how the unconscious DNA of the organization works.

To illustrate this, consider for a moment the intriguing habitual behaviour demonstrated by monkeys in The Monkey Story, which is about an experiment with five monkeys locked in a cage with a ladder leading towards the top, and a banana hung from the ceiling above. The following is an extract from *Business Exposed* by Professor Freek Vermeulen[1].

 *"... One of the monkeys would race towards the ladder, intending to climb it and grab the banana. However, as soon as he would start to climb, the scientist would spray the monkey with ice-cold water. In addition, he would also spray the other four monkeys ...*

When a second monkey was about to climb the ladder, again the scientist would spray the monkey with ice-cold water, and apply the same treatment to its four fellow inmates; likewise for the third climber and, if they were particularly persistent, the fourth one. Then they would have learned their lesson: they were not going to climb the ladder again – banana or no banana.

In order to gain further pleasure or, I guess, prolong the experiment, the scientist outside the cage would then replace one of the monkeys with a new one. As can be expected, the new guy would spot the banana, think 'why don't these idiots go get it?!' and start climbing the ladder. Then, however, it got interesting: the other four monkeys, familiar with the cold-water treatment, would run towards the new guy – and beat him up.

The new guy, blissfully unaware of the cold-water history, would get the message: no climbing up the ladder in this cage – banana or no banana.

---

[1] *Source: Business Exposed* – Professor Freek Vermeulen, Oct. 2010.

[They then continued to replace one monkey after another until] ... a new monkey was introduced into the cage. It ran toward the ladder only to get beaten up by the others. Yet, this monkey turned around and asked 'why do you beat me up when I try to get the banana?' The other four monkeys stopped, looked at each other slightly puzzled and, finally, shrugged their shoulders: 'Don't know. But that's the way we do things around here'... "

What this story illustrates is that all organizations develop habits and ways of working that become routine and the way we do things around here – this is the organization's culture or DNA whose purpose is to lock in specific behaviours and actions. The key challenge for you is to be able to stand outside your organization's DNA to observe it afresh and challenge where it is hindering progress – this is a high class ability!

Break unconscious addictions

The unconscious addiction we have in our organizations to continue doing things the way we always have is an automatic response that takes control of us! We are looking to surface this and break it once and for all.

Leaders need to help their people to break free from their past experience and inhibitors, because these usually only stand in the way of impactful and sustainable change. This is achieved by uncovering the context, confronting past experience where necessary and looking at the "real" conversations people are having.

> "People need to come together and be exposed to an environment that encourages open discussion."

People need to come together and be exposed to an environment that encourages open discussion. Once views, opinions, challenges and concerns have been shared, a basis for alignment will emerge and commitment to change can be gained.

> "No problem can be solved from the same level of consciousness that created it."
>
> *Albert Einstein*

What is needed at this point is concerted training and development that will give you the ability to fundamentally transform their context. This in turn will allow people freedom to explore ideas and ambitions that would have previously been considered impossible, so they can make their ideas reality in a short time frame. Without these new ways of thinking and acting, you are resigned to trying to solve the problems from inside the box of existing mindsets.

Unconscious DNA is critical

Organizational DNA creates what is good, bad, celebrated, rejected. It sets the expectations of the company and unconsciously guides the ways of working and habitual behaviour and rituals.

Other challenges embedded within the DNA of an organization show up as follows:

- An unconscious way of being successful:
    - If you don't know it you can't expose it.
    - Underlying assumptions that guide actions.
- A natural power base that has evolved within the organization:
    - This might reside in a specific department, region or level of the hierarchy.
    - Certain personality types may be revered.

How to cut through the DNA

To start to disrupt the previously successful (but now limiting) perspectives of an organization and its people, here's how you must change:

From Leaders:	To Leaders:
• Living with limiting habits and rituals.	• Breaking limiting beliefs and assumptions.
• Constrained by history, such as previous strategies.	• Committed to driving changes in mindsets and behaviour.
• Blind to limitations and stuck in the box.	• Aware of limits and choosing at will to work outside of them.
• Playing politics.	• Taking decisions based on what's best for the organization.
• Conforming to Organizational frameworks.	• Stepping away from the norm.

Handle structural challenges

Organizational structures play an important role in the performance of any organization. The various forms of ownership have different influences in terms of culture, behaviour, drivers and process, depending on the model.

All organizations exhibit this, including:

- Plc versus private equity
- subsidiary versus head office
- matrix and regional structures.

The type of organization you operate in is actually irrelevant. There will be differences in these environments, but one thing remains the same – people need to recognize what these structures require to make them successful. There will be differences that arise that must be considered. Certain organizational structures will perform tasks better than others depending on their overall aims and objectives.

An organization's ownership will lead to differing behaviours and characteristics in the delivery of business performance and change. For example, let's discuss private equity (PE) in comparison to a public limited company (Plc), where some behaviours and characteristics are common, some similar and some completely different due to the aims and approaches to executing the organization's objectives.

It should be noted that in other organizations, whether it is manufacturing, retailing or public sectors, similar differences will be seen.

The table below looks at different characteristics (e.g. natural desire for performance in PE with corresponding clarity of purpose and incentives) and the differences that exist in Plc business environments.

PLC VERSUS PE – CONTEXT FOR LEADERSHIP

PE	Plc
• Clarity of purpose. • Cost/benefit analysis is clear. • Positive attitude to risk. • Responsive (shorter decision making). • Clear incentives to be entrepreneurial and perform well.	• Purpose less clear – historically driven? • Priority to protect brand/reputation. • Negative attitude to risk. • Decision making hierarchical/drawn out? • Job security and "safe pairs of hands" valued.

Understanding differences and how to deliver change in these environments is important. It requires leaders to identify and work with the DNA in these differing business environments. The various forms of ownership have different influences on leadership behaviour. For the purpose of providing meaningful examples of the different leadership challenges and the different relationships generated within and across the organization, the Plc and PE ownership models will be discussed in more depth to highlight potential challenges.

COMPARING THE PLC AND PE MODELS

Plc organizations are generally guided by their legacy. Plc operating routines are generally strong, if not sometimes rigid. In many instances, if all the senior management were to leave, the company would continue doing the things it knows how to do without disruption. Business performance would probably drift over time, but nothing is likely to happen in the short term. In many situations, the strength of the company's brand or reputation provides protection.

> "The more risk adverse, the lower the ambition."

The bigger the company, the more it may try and protect its brand and reputation rather than change, even when change could positively improve performance and results. Initiating and mobilizing change in a large and complex organization is going to be challenging. Attitude to change has a direct influence on the ambition of the company to make shifts in the business. "The more risk adverse, the lower the ambition" is a sweeping statement. However, the statement does provide the context for assessing the management's likely commitment to change. For example, a change to restructure an airport terminal layout to improve queuing at check-in desks is unlikely to be received well when the baggage handlers are on strike for pay and the airport has been closed. There would be more important short term priorities. When the issues of today have been resolved, the organization will be more receptive, even though logically today may be the best time to reorganize the airport whilst it is empty.

> "The bigger the company, the more it may try and protect its brand and reputation rather than change."

Once change has been accepted, the need for continuous organizational alignment is important. This will require good supporting information for selling each phase of the change, up-to-date and regular communication and a process to keep the organization aligned with the change as it progresses (specifically, but not limited to, those directly involved).

Due to political networks and complexity arising from a matrix organization, powerful commentators, conflicting objectives and lack of clarity at the middle and lower levels of the organization will exist.

Our experience has shown that people need to be prepared for change so that the organization is "fit for purpose". In smaller as well as larger organizations, bringing people together to discuss issues and engage them in what appears to them to be difficult situations both present and future needs to become routine.

If not, it is highly likely that the organization will quickly run out of alignment and change will slow and possibly stop. As you may have experienced, busy organizations develop new and exciting initiatives on a frequent basis. If alignment is not maintained, even an important change can lose its profile and pace as people switch their attention to the next up and coming project. These organizational characteristics and associated behaviours must be recognized and managed. The importance of continuous organizational alignment is often overlooked.

In the public eye, PE companies are seen as higher risk environments with higher returns on investments from successful examples, but also unwelcome losses from failures. However, the private equity environment raises confidence and enthusiasm for change. Both the potential rewards and clarity of purpose and objectives provide stronger motivations that positively influence the management's assessment and subsequent management of business risks. Plc companies do not have this clarity of purpose and the management of risk can be amplified, bringing a greater emphasis on concerns of poor performance or disruption during a period of change.

Private equity is not promoted as the ideal solution as it does carry drawbacks whereby its focus on performance can lead to short-term thinking and possibly taking bigger than necessary risks. PE environments are often cited as lean and mean, but they still need to be fit for purpose to manage change and that is consistent with all organizations.

CONSIDERATIONS WHEN ASSESSING DNA USING OUR COMPANY OWNERSHIP EXAMPLES

The learning from both ownership examples relates to understanding the DNA in each environment and the corresponding approach to change and how to manage it before and during the related shift that will take place.

Both ownership models generally introduce risk management processes, but in private equity in general the environment is less risk adverse. There is clarity of purpose and their staff can understand more clearly the targets of the company and why change is needed. Due to shorter and quicker routes for decisions and communication, alignment between management is easier and more effective.

There is no right or wrong with differing ownership models, although the working environments can be very different, as discussed.

Therefore, it is advised that leaders and change managers consider:

- The need for frequent and up-to-date communication to avoid the power of commentators slowing or stopping progress. Also, avoid new and perceived to be more up-to-date projects taking away the engagement in change (especially in large and complex organizations that are guided by the past).
- Assess the DNA and the current context within the business to ensure change is presented at a time when it will be accepted and be given the right level of importance.
- Ensure that alignment of management and staff across the organization is not considered as a one-time event. It should be continuous.

- Clarity of purpose and objectives, rewards and related methods of motivation as seen in PE will help engagement and the ongoing participation and interest of stakeholders.

Once leaders and change agents have recognized, embraced and prepared for the above it allows for new ways of thinking and a new approach.

Leaders typically face additional force fields in the form of structural challenges within their organizations:

- Playing politics in the hierarchy (this determines what people can and can't do).
- Prioritizing hierarchy over the objectives of the organization.
- Assumptions about the perceived capabilities of certain functions and/or divisions.

In a similar way, these force fields must be managed to avoid delays in progress.

Bringing the unconscious DNA to the surface

The challenge

A global leader in FMCG recognized that they had a burning platform. For the last two years, management had been desperately trying to wake the organization up, to change behaviour and to promote taking ownership of information, as well as being accountable for their commercial objectives in the context of some significant up and coming competitive challenges.

The organization gave growth and profit returns of 7% year in year out, and it was very happy with those returns. However, the organization had become complacent as a result of normalizing this situation. Despite this, their market place was becoming more competitive, and it was getting harder and harder to win business.

Those 7% returns were under serious threat. Efforts to make people more empowered and ambitious were falling short – the existing DNA meant that people only committed to what they thought they could deliver, as they had never missed plan. The leadership had not seen the need for change as each year the results were "ok".

What this meant in practice was that the organization looked historically at what they could do and then committed to this level of performance, rather than being more ambitious and trying new things in order to win in the changing market place. As time went on, the unconscious DNA that had worked well for so long started to backfire – and the company came under threat as they were unable to break through the status quo.

The approach

Through extensive development and working with the leaders and managers, we were able to surface the unconscious DNA, habits and rituals that were limiting the organization. Once people were aware of these, they were prepared to deal with the perceived risks and force fields in the organization and to work outside of them. The management teams set bold challenges that were designed to have the organization achieve extraordinary results. These in turn liberated the organization to try new approaches, be innovative, get creative and once again lead their industry.

The results

The organization started to produce results previously considered impossible. Before this understanding, they had only ever committed to what they could accomplish – they were constrained by history. These results were in an area of new product innovation that was 50% quicker to market and in market penetration, increasing market share gain significantly by double digits.

Once leaders were eventually unconstrained by the myths and conclusions the organization was built upon, they were able to create a breakthrough strategy, vision and direction for the organization. This was ambitious, and it has been welcomed. People can now see the limits of how they were working previously; once you can see it, you can let go of it.

What enabled the shifts and the success?

This case study illustrates the power of confronting the organizational DNA, habits and ways of operating that have made the company successful. By doing this, the organization had the choice to work outside of these constraints. They coupled this freedom with setting breakthrough challenges, which by design had the organization confront the things that limited their thinking. The effect was like dynamite! People were liberated from "the history" to take bold action in line with a future they were excited and energized about. What if this could become the default for the organization?

Key takeaway practices

• Look to surface the conventional wisdom, assumptions and beliefs that are blocking the objectives and challenges you have.
• Make people aware of the unconscious DNA in the organization and how it affects the actions they take and don't take.
• Have people challenge these assumptions.
• Practise flipping the thinking and imagining what you would do if you had no limits.

"Twenty years from now you will be more disappointed by the things that you didn't do than by the ones you did do. So throw off the bowlines. Sail away from the safe harbor. Catch the trade winds in your sails. Explore. Dream. Discover."

H. Jackson Brown Jr, *P.S. I Love You*

Shift 6

KEEPING THE ORGANIZATION FUTURE-FOCUSED

To keep the organization future-focused, you need to create structures that ensure the new aspirations can be achieved.

Know the power of conversation

It is critical to understand the true power of conversation.

There is a common belief among individuals and society that "talk is cheap", and we have probably all heard the phrase "actions speak louder than words". The fundamental assumption here is that "what you say doesn't really matter", because action is what matters. This is a fallacy. How we talk and listen determines both our actions and the actions of the people around us. Action follows the way we speak, listen and think.

> "How we talk and listen determines both our actions and the actions of the people around us."

A good example is that of a sales convention held by a well-known global FMCG organization. Picture a professional stage, dry-ice, big music and theatrical introductions. Then add a high-energy speech from the Sales Director encouraging his teams to strive for 50% growth with the promise of better cars, bigger bonuses and slick new phones. Naturally, the sales teams are highly motivated, and there is positive energy buzzing and momentum built around this breakthrough target.

Later on that day, during evening drinks, the Sales Director lets it slip that in fact, "10% growth would be just great, guys". This smashes the context that had been built up earlier and constructs a new reality – "10% is what is really expected". Sure enough, at the end of each quarter over the next 12 months, the sales for that year were re-forecast. The company delivered 9% sales growth.

It's obvious that words matter – what a leader says can lead to an unintended consequence inconsistent with the results you want. For example, comments after a difficult conversation with a colleague or reflections on their own levels of possibility for the company.

What people say creates reality. For example, when the boss says, "You are fired" you experience a major shift in your reality; just as when the vicar says, "You are married" – or a Prime Minister says, "We are at war". Consider the reality that you want to build in the minds of your people – do your words reflect your ambitions? Let's consider an example of a negotiation, if you were selling an item for £100 and were committed to getting this, then you would need to act consistently with that objective. In this example, if you discuss the price with a potential buyer and receive a counter-offer and you change your price expectation to bridge the gap, the buyer will immediately know that you have shifted once and there is a high probability that you will do so again. The negotiation will continue. The lesson here is even when you are making a stand for change, once you shift, people will think about compromise and how they can bridge the gap between today's reality and tomorrow – your vision immediately starts to be diluted.

"What people say creates reality."

A leader's role and what that leader says are pivotal in training teams to speak and think from the future. Consider typical conversations held at a major sporting event, such as a football match. There is a key difference between the conversations of the commentators and the conversations the coach has with the team.

Leaders need to consider themselves as the coach; always thinking about how to get the best out of their team. They should be having conversations about how to win and how to move the game forward, not being influenced by conversations at the sidelines, speculation and general commentary.

In organizations, minute by minute, moment by moment, we are either commentating on some kind of mediocrity based on the past or coaching ourselves to some kind of future we want. These are two fundamentally different paradigms, as illustrated in the following diagram.

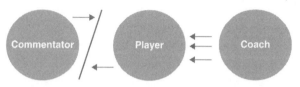

Conventional Thinking		**Breakthrough Thinking**
A future created by your past		*A future free from the past*
Past interpretations	**Present actions**	**Future possibilities**
Assessments	Facts	Visions
Opinions	Promises and request	Commitments
Judgements		
Stories		
I think ...	The facts are ...	I declare ...
My opinion/view is ...	I promise to ...	I'm committed to ...
I agree/don't agree ...	I request that you ...	What's possible is ...
The evidence shows	I can't do this, but can	We are capable of ...
that ...	do ...	

Action follows both commentating and coaching. However, coaching conversations produce fundamentally different actions. When someone has a new project or initiative, people will often give you a commentary on why it is difficult to accomplish. This is only natural. Yet the action that people take in the face of this commentary generally leads to continuous improvement, but not extraordinary results.

Interestingly, a number of studies have indicated that a large proportion (>80%) of conversations in the Western world are based on commentating not actions and possibilities.

Make strong commitments

Leading your organization to remain in a future that is liberated from the past also involves making strong commitments and declarations about current and future actions.

WHAT DO COMMITTED PEOPLE SAY AND DO?

People who are committed to achieving breakthrough results hold a different kind of conversation, following the principles outlined below:

Conventional Conversation	Breakthrough Conversation
• Considers process. • Is concerned with search and discovery. • Is based on black and white and immediate judgement (yes/no, right/wrong, true/false, either/or). • Sets up dichotomies and contradictions to force a choice or decision. • Believes that information and judgement are enough. • Seeks to explain. • Describes and reports, and talks about change. • Asks "what's wrong or lacking?" • Seeks the right process. • Uses adversarial argument to explore a subject	• Considers results. • Is concerned with design and invention. • Explores possibilities without drawing premature conclusions. • Embraces both sides of a contradiction, and seeks to design a way forward. • Deliberately generates new ideas and new concepts. • Seeks to initiate. • Generates change. • Asks "what's missing and how can I provide it?" • Seeks the result. • Uses a subject cooperatively, with a willingness to be surprised.

People who are committed to a future free from the past will avoid having conversations based upon assessments, opinions and justifications. Instead, they will typically make statements such as:

- "I'm committed to ..."
- "What's possible is ..."
- "We are capable of ..."

Commentators can be a power force field in an organization – to such an extent that a company strategy or desired direction freezes. The situation often leads to an organization being very busy but with little or no alignment or focus; basically standing still and remaining in a static or frozen state – often described as stability. The bigger an organization or company becomes, the more likely this situation will arise.

> "As the fear of loss is generally greater than the desire for gain, staying in the frozen state requires little convincing."

Different work environments can be more effective in gaining an organization's alignment and focus in delivering a new and exciting vision. However, often the organization will need to be unfrozen to enable progress. In a frozen state the commentators play a lead role in expressing all the risks associated with any proposed change. As the fear of loss is generally greater than the desire for gain, staying in the frozen state requires little convincing.

UNFREEZING AN ORGANIZATION

Consider when a company is acquired, a school is integrated with an adjacent district or county, or a hospital is transferred under the management of a new healthcare trust. In these situations the organization becomes unfrozen and during that time will be more accepting of change.

Now let's take this matter a little deeper and consider an acquisition that involves all or part of a business moving under the new ownership.

On the day the organization is acquired and the name above the main entrance is changed, this does not constitute an immediate change of behaviour, mindset or a new way of working. However, it is one event that initiates the unfreezing of the organization. Speculation about the future begins and staff start to build a future in their minds based on the limited and often inaccurate information they have to hand. Whether the change involves a large or small organization a similar situation generally occurs.

The organization now starts to unfreeze and prepare itself for a change based on personal insights and opinions of staff. Few organizations take the opportunity during a period when an organization is unfrozen to make significant changes, yet staff are preparing themselves for a different world.

"Few organizations take the opportunity during a period when the organization is unfrozen to make significant changes, yet staff are preparing themselves for a different world."

Initially when a company is acquired management may create a bold vision set between executives and key management. It is relatively easy at this point in time to be optimistic; however, as time progresses conditions and constraints begin to influence management's thinking. The need for an easy life creeps in. Commentators see all the risks.

Significant opportunity can be missed, as staff are expecting something different to happen and generally their expectations go way beyond what is finally planned. Staff continue to build a picture in their mind of a new state following change, talking at coffee machines and building on each other's views and opinions. In most cases they are not informed sufficiently and therefore their thinking is not constrained by any real constraints.

In these situations, the worst is feared or the best assumed and staff are prepared for the extremes. In the meantime, management is working hard to minimize disruption, tighten controls and avoid risk.

There quickly becomes a misalignment of expectations, which can cause delays and relatively poor results. This is a period when cool heads with ambition and fresh thinking can create a platform for rapid change, building organizational muscle on the journey to a new and more dynamic business model.

Whilst management fear instability, they are also concerned about putting their business with customers at risk. It is important that management do not underestimate the capability of the organization to keep the wheels of the business turning. The risk is likely to be lower than perceived.

Business routines will continue; the paradigm is strong and it naturally creates sustainability in the day-to-day requirements for servicing its customers.

The risk associated with poor ambition of management is that the organization freezes again. If the organization freezes, it can be a 12-month process to create an environment that provides a similar context for change.

Change in ownership

The challenge

A PE backed company was acquired by a Plc. Generally this acquisition could be described as two competitors coming together. The market was and still is highly competitive. The new owners set the objective to have a professional and controlled integration of the two companies to help manage risk.

The approach

To this end, the new owners asserted that both companies would continue to compete (rather than integrate). This would slow down the integration process but enable stability and a more controlled move to a new state (one company). However, commercial teams could not continue effectively as competitors as the context had changed.

For example, customers were pushing for a more rapid integration to streamline their interfaces with the new company. In addition, the acquired company felt uncomfortable competing with the sales team from the acquiring company soon to be their new colleagues. The company's sales performance started to come under pressure because sales staff were trying to foster new relationships with the new owners and were watching as integration of less business critical back offices was being planned. Focus was lost. Confusion reigned. The company was unfrozen.

Commentators from both companies started to create stories about why the organizations were finding it difficult and business was being negatively impacted. For example, we acquired this company and they are not as good as we were told: "look at the performance now". Conversely, the acquired teams were citing poor communication to customers with claims from competing sales staff that "the acquired company would soon have its products removed from sale as many were not required in the future".

This situation created an impossible working environment, where staff were trying to accelerate the integration of both companies, yet being asked to compete with each other until the official integration could commence. This led to each company's sales teams remaining competitors in the market until integration meant they were no longer enemies anymore! This all happened because management were worried about the risks, and decided to keep the organizations separate until they could find a better way and a less risky time to put them together.

The organizations became unfrozen as a result of the change in ownership, yet management was trying to still operate in the previous frozen state. There was a clear misalignment between management and staff.

There was concern about integration, so going slower appeared more sensible. However, the staff couldn't cope and became very frustrated. They wanted to go faster and move to a new and more exciting state with all the benefits of the newly formed organization. Staff could see customers getting confused because they didn't understand what the future looked like and whilst the two companies were still competing there was no clear picture of the future for them.

The results

When the organization did finally integrate, the process was smooth with little or no disruption in relation to the scale and complexity to be managed. So much was changed quickly because everybody was ready for change. Management got in the way of change because they were frightened of losing control. Nobody was the winner during this period.

This case study highlights much of the learning from this section. Unfrozen organizations can, if given the freedom, help to deliver a bold new future. Staff are prepared for change and will help the change move quickly and effectively if alignment with management objectives is reached quickly. Otherwise the road ahead can be severely challenged, with commentators creating unhelpful and often disruptive stories all leading to a lot of frustrated people.

Key Takeaway Practices

• Recognize the different conversations people are having. Are they anchored in the past, present or future? Ask questions to move people to the future state.

• Turn concerns into identifying what is missing and requests – this always moves things forwards.

• Manage conversations – turning past interpretations to future possibility.

• Have new sets of conversations:

  • Imagine you have already achieved the goal: how did it happen?

  • Focus on what is happening versus stories.

  • Identify what the commitment is and what is missing.

• Make bold promises and requests to put yourself and others to the test.

"You can't connect the dots looking forward; you can only connect them looking backwards. So you have to trust that the dots will somehow connect in your future. You have to trust in something - your gut, destiny, life, karma, whatever. This approach has never let me down, and it has made all the difference in my life."

Steve Jobs

GAINING ENERGY FROM SETBACKS

To achieve something extraordinary, there is *always a gap* between the current reality and the possibility we have committed to.

That pathway to commitment is paved with continual setbacks that need to be overcome, yet as human beings we tend to perceive these setbacks as problems and something "bad" – which we then try to avoid. This is an issue as the more ambitious you are, the more setbacks you will have.

In most organizations people are excellent at setting goals and objectives.

> "No amount of incremental change can turn a propeller engine into a jet. This shift is transformation."

But then they hit a brick wall, rationalize the situation, justify why it is that way and then set a new goal and objective – usually a lower one. This is the path of least resistance that leads to incremental improvement, as opposed to extraordinary results.

As you may already realize, no amount of incremental change can turn a propeller engine into a jet. This shift is transformation. The concept of a jet engine is completely different. This example illustrates how a shift in thinking led to something extraordinary at the time.

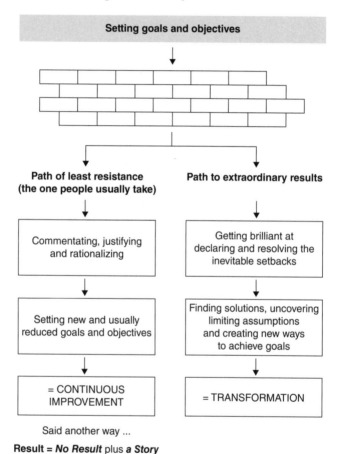

Setting goals and objectives

Path of least resistance (the one people usually take)

Commentating, justifying and rationalizing

↓

Setting new and usually reduced goals and objectives

↓

= CONTINUOUS IMPROVEMENT

Path to extraordinary results

Getting brilliant at declaring and resolving the inevitable setbacks

↓

Finding solutions, uncovering limiting assumptions and creating new ways to achieve goals

↓

= TRANSFORMATION

Said another way ...

Result = *No Result* plus *a Story* about why there's no result

There is a fundamental difference in the way that we perceive and deal with problems required here:

Conventional Approach	Breakthrough Approach
• Perceiving and focusing on problems.	• Perceiving and handling setbacks.
• Not seeking out problems.	• Actively looking for where setbacks might happen.
• Being upset when problems occur – "We shouldn't have problems".	• Expecting and embracing setbacks – they are often the source of breakthroughs.
• Focus on whose fault the problem is – you, me, it ...	• Use setbacks to build understanding of each other and to learn.
• Actions are driven by perceptions and your commentary.	• Actions are driven by your commitment.
• Take time to recover or change the goal so that you are still "on target".	• Remain focused on the desired outcome, and how this can be achieved within the original timeframe and scope.

Stopping setbacks from limiting results

Gaining energy from setbacks is the antidote to normalizing. When a new commitment is made to an extraordinary result and the first setbacks show up, the response can very often be negative:

• People lose touch with the original bold commitment and start to argue about what they should be committed to and how they should do things – rather than getting on with doing what's needed to meet the original commitment.

• People become daunted by the issues that need to be resolved, and fall back on what they know, doing what they have done before. Hence, they are captured by the beliefs and assumptions they have always held: this is conventional wisdom and DNA taking hold.

• People decide that they can't meet the commitment, and turn their attention to justifying and rationalizing that decision and negotiating a new, less bold commitment. They are quick to point out what's wrong to anyone who disagrees, and they begin to believe they must have been crazy to make the commitment in the first place!

As a result they become trapped in their beliefs, assumptions and opinions about:

• What's the right commitment (what works).
• What's now important.
• What's unlikely and what doesn't work.
• What's obvious for them.
• What's the right way to do things, the way that is normal.
• What's the wrong way to do things (what has previously failed).
• What's the best way to do things (what we know previously worked).
• What they agree with and what they think is not true.

ORGANIZATIONS AND SETBACKS

Organizations can behave in different ways as they begin to face up to setbacks.

Commentators start to anticipate and expand on the potential issues and challenges to the point that they are almost dreaming up problems. People can be very creative in developing obstacles in their mind and then become very focused on developing justification and supporting anecdotal or even factual evidence to engage others in their thoughts. Of course, at this point in time, all such challenges will only be speculation based and views, opinions and assumptions that anticipate the future in a very convincing way for others.

Another situation may be that decision makers introduce ongoing delays. It may be the case that they are becoming uncertain about their commitments due to a recently known impact of the change either on them as individuals or on their function. When this happens setbacks feed prolonged procrastination.

For example, more analysis may be sought by project groups or senior management. Additional steps in the change programme are introduced for what are believed to be better decisions to secure a more successful outcome. Another delaying tactic is senior management putting on hold a change due to anticipated market forces. For example, if a good Christmas trading period is required to secure the annual budgets, corresponding action may be to have all staff focused on this budget objective and then revert back to the change project once the trading period has passed. You may guess what happens next, once Christmas is over, Easter is rapidly approaching and the change project is put back further. This type of action avoids leaders being embarrassed due to their lack of confidence or resistance to change.

Both the above situations created by commentators and procrastination will naturally arise and create emotional engagement with those in the organization. This situation will need managing.

It is only natural for us to stand behind our beliefs, assumptions and opinions – we are only human. We are operating in the way we have always done, informed by our past. We are trying our best to deliver predictable results safely, securely and responsibly. We deal with setbacks by falling back on what we know. What we know is only based on our past experience, our assumptions and our conclusions about what's happening around us now.

One way to help avoid some of these setbacks in organizations is to consider the following points:

- Maintain regular communication and maintain alignment across those engaged in the change. At the beginning of a change, alignment is likely to be reached as the impact on those involved is low, i.e. nothing has yet happened. Do not expect alignment to continue. The probability of that happening is small. Good communication on progress and associated problem resolution will help, but do not expect that to continue. The commentators and procrastination actions will be addressed and challenged regularly.

• Avoid righteousness statements or claims that only feed power into the arguments being set against a change.

Remember that challenging commentators are seldom the decision makers, but their actions lead to the power to delay being passed to them. There are many times when commentators should be thanked for their opinions and you continue to move forward without changing your plans. Don't allow their approach to delay you if their comments are not relevant or important.

Of course if the commentator has a senior position within the organization, that may require a professional approach to closing down their actions. Listen, evaluate if there is any learning from their comments and then take any appropriate action, or do nothing, depending on what is required.

Our beliefs may be out of date, just as the commentators may be ill-informed. Our beliefs certainly cannot be informed by what we don't know, and our assumptions and conclusions about what's happening now may be inaccurate. What's needed may be completely untested. We can be sure that Sir Frank Whittle did not have all the answers enabling him to deliver his vision to develop the jet engine. He experienced many breakthroughs that created shifts in the thinking and confidence of others. Each step forward helped to convince others of his vision and to finally deliver a working jet engine.

Shift your attention

Breakthroughs happen when we shift how we are thinking. We need to operate from a viewpoint and belief that:

- Our bold commitment is possible and can always be created. Everything necessary to make it real exists in the world.
- We are accountable for the result, and we are capable of making it happen.
- Nothing is fixed apart from what we are committed to, the natural laws of the world and what we need to do to stay legal.
- Everything else can be challenged.

This means rejecting *should*, *shouldn't*, *can't* and any other *opinions* that are inconsistent with our commitment.

Truly being committed means creating empowering new must dos, consistent with our commitment.

For each must do, look at what is already in place, and what is missing and essential. Then focus your efforts on finding or creating that which is missing. This very simple shift of attention from why something is not possible to seeking out that which makes it possible creates miraculous results over and over again.

> "For each must do, look at what is already in place, and what is missing and essential."

What usually stops action on must dos, is that until our alternative beliefs and assumptions are surfaced, they are invisible to us. We have strong opinions and conclusions and hold them as true – giving us no room to be creative.

One of the main obstacles to seeking out what is missing and essential is the feeling that something is impossible or requires so much to be done. At this point our vision turns into something that conceptually is attractive but in our reality is far too much trouble to manage or commit to. All the wrong emotions start to play lead roles in our minds.

To illustrate this emotional state of mind and the role it plays, try and think back to a time whilst at work or home when you had what appeared in front of you to be a large amount of work with many actions to be done. It might be a long list of emails to answer that keeps growing. As you feel overwhelmed you delay action and the problem keeps growing. After a period of procrastination you decide to tackle the problem head on. Within no time at all you get through the workload and wonder how you could have completed the task(s) so quickly. What was all the worry about? Feelings of achievement and success are also high after the event.

Although this is a trivial example compared to delivering a big and bold vision, it is similar emotions that hold us back from the bigger things in life. Such as starting our own business or moving to live and work in another country.

The lesson is that you have to try. Don't put off until tomorrow what can be done today is a very profound saying. Too often we look into the past or into the future and forget about the present. We can only get things done in the present.

> "Too often we look into the past or into the future and forget about the present."

Operating from a commitment way beyond a predictable result is a scary place to be – and can even feel irresponsible. The associated emotions are not simple to overcome. Managing the associated feelings is related to how you assess risk, which can be helped with a skilled coach, mentor or facilitator if a wider group is involved. Such conversations allow you to analyse the risk and highlight the specific areas that need addressing, to help mitigate initial negative reactions that leads to eliminating unnecessary concerns. Risks generally show up bigger when you start out!

How to gain energy from setbacks

You should aim to demonstrate to your organization a dramatic shift. Perhaps a shift away from how they would normally solve problems. This approach will "give permission" to people to do the same.

"From" Leaders:	"To" Leaders:
• Seeing problems as "wrong" or too risky without any further investigation. This change shouldn't happen; something to be avoided.	• Embracing setbacks as they show us the limits of our current thinking. • Knowing that the pathway to breakthroughs is addressing constant setbacks. • A leader's positive and proactive approach to setbacks demonstrates to other people that resolutions are possible and that the vision is becoming and can be a reality.

Restoring trust in a long-term partnership

A high profile clinical study for a critical new product had been struggling to meet timelines for 18 months. Critical patient recruitment was running 60% behind targets. The study was being delivered in full by a Clinical Research Organization (CRO) in partnership with the pharmaceutical company and stakes were high for both parties. Failure would very likely jeopardize long-term strategic ambitions and severely negatively impact the overall valuation of the pharmaceutical company.

Relationships had broken down in the study team, and frustration was high. This was causing a threat to the continuation of the study in its existing form. The belief about the study was that "this is impossible to recover" – but it all turned around in just five months.

The challenge

Both organizations had taken steps to get the study back on track, but the underlying "this is impossible" belief, together with doubt, blame, lack of trust and limited resources on both sides meant that nobody could envisage results being delivered. The challenge was to shift this context to one that drove true partnership behaviour and breakthrough delivery within constrained resources.

The three main challenges were:

1. To let go of the history, and have people see their personal responsibility for creating change, refocusing the team context to working in partnership, being proactive and managing setbacks effectively.
2. To create a study team for patient recruitment targets, capable of delivering the required outcome at breakthrough pace.

3. To reinstate the confidence and belief in success in both organizations with all key stakeholders.

The approach

Our approach followed three critical steps over a period of five months:

1. Pre-work dialogue with individual stakeholders.
    • Assessing the gravity of people's concerns and their appetite for a new possible future of successful partnership and delivery.
    • Creating a conversation about their future ambitions for the study.
2. Strategic partnering programme.
    • Giving the team the tools to partner with one another.
    • Creating the ability to generate a commitment and align behind it for a completely different future.
    • Instilling skills to create innovative solutions and ways of working that stepped outside conventional thinking and acting.
    • Both companies appointed near full-time programme managers to hold the joint team accountable for commitments and promises, with a direct line of sight to senior management.

3. Breakthrough coaching of key people in the study's team and in meetings to support live scenarios in the day-to-day operations.

The results

All breakthrough milestone goals were achieved over a five-month period.

Trust was restored, and subsequent agreements were made to reduce operational input and checks by the pharmaceutical organization. The study had been established for 18 months with these changes enabled the following results:

- Patient recruitment rose from 650 to 10,000 patients to hit a critical milestone in just five months.
- There was a 200% change in the pace of site initiations per month: from an average of 10 to 20 a month in only three months. This was sustained, leading to 207 global sites being initiated into the study (from the previous 134) over five months – and coming in at the original target set out at the beginning of the study.
- Both organizations challenged existing protocol and created new processes, developing a new approach based on mutual trust and alignment.

- The team's way of working is now characterized by trust, empowerment, innovation and joint responsibility. To quote: "These study meetings have completely changed; it feels a pleasure to attend the meeting now!"
- These results restored confidence and renewed both organizations' strategic ambitions for a long-term partnership.

Key takeaway practices

- Actively look for setbacks and ask what is missing to achieve the commitment.
- Watch and intervene in the rationalizing process that you and your colleagues may start to go through.
- Create an environment where people can bring up the potential and actual setbacks freely and challenge assumptions.
- See setbacks as the pathway to extraordinary outcomes.

SUMMARY

In 2013, a new international company was born as a result of the acquisition of a private equity-based firm. The existing private equity business was merged with the international business of a Japanese manufacturer.

The first senior management conference was held in Himeji, Japan, bringing together around 70 executive managers of the company. The event was designed around taking the management teams through a process to improve their personal and group performance. Individuals in the room came from approximately 15 different countries, and almost the same number of languages was spoken.

This story illustrates the relevance of the Magnificent Seven shifts in achieving a new world record.

The Magnificent Seven shifts in action

THE CHALLENGE

The focus for this event was to bring teams from two previously autonomous companies together and to explore possible ways of managing the newly merged company, given the diverse cultures, nationalities and language barriers.

There was much apprehension about the merger, and many perceived risks were rising to the surface, for example:

- Research shows that very few mergers of Western and Japanese companies are successful.
- How would the desire for perfection demonstrated in Japanese culture fit with a company whose growth agenda placed entrepreneurs in the front line of the business?
- How would the manufacturing-based culture of the Japanese team fit with the sales, service-based culture of the Western company?
- Those from the private equity-based company thrived on performance and results and were previously highly incentivized financially. The Japanese mindset was focused on the long term and less on the results of today, incentivized by "jobs for life".
- How could good communication in English be ensured with so few native English speakers? Communication and alignment of teams would be very different.

The teams were aware that during the event we would be attempting to break a world record for the largest number of people who could sit on the floor cross-legged, link arms and all stand up simultaneously – all facing forwards! This feat may sound easy, but it was in fact very difficult. The difference in people's height, leg strength and coordination, not forgetting the ability to stand up without the use of your hands from a seated cross-legged position, all combined to present a real challenge!

THE APPROACH

Before the event, a team consisting of a few of the company's top Swiss engineers was tasked with thinking through our approach. This team recorded their attempts to achieve the goal with around 15 people, and not the required 42 or more. They failed, but they made progress in eliminating some of the approaches that didn't work well.

Shift 1: Letting go of the past

The teams needed to let go of the strong commentary leading up to the event. This said that the whole thing was "a waste of time", and that the world record attempt in particular was "childish" and not achievable.

Many people were concerned about being embarrassed about failing and couldn't see the possibility of success, especially given the challenge of so many different languages being spoken.

The world record attempt had to be completed successfully on the day of the conference in front of judges from the Guinness Book of Records, in the two hours allotted for the exercise.

As the time approached for our two-hour slot, we had no confirmed leader, although the direction was to be set by the senior engineer tasked to prepare our approach. There were about 70 people present, and as you may imagine they all started to form little groups, testing their ability to sit and stand cross-legged in tandem. People were falling around on the floor, nobody was succeeding and whilst there was positive energy bouncing from the walls, no actual progress was being made. Quite simply, it was chaos!

To achieve Shift 1: Letting go of the past, people had to change their viewpoint. There were egos at play. Many people perceived themselves to be technical experts in specific fields and were of a *serious mindset*, which did not fit with the task in hand. Many didn't like being told what to do, evidencing "it's not the way we do things around here".

Shift 2: Developing breakthrough ambition

A new frame of reference had to be developed for people; a new context created around what we were aiming to do and why. This was totally unknown territory, and it was certainly not predictable. We didn't know if we could do this, even on the day itself.

The CEO gave the senior engineer his support to try and coordinate the team. People started to form groups designated to complete specific tasks. Again, this failed – although the positive energy was maintained.

The world record was being performed in the company's head office and by now the president of the investment company had arrived to watch our progress. He brought with him other Japanese senior executives. The visitors couldn't believe what they were seeing.

Shift 3: Creating a bold new future

The focus for this event was to bring together teams from the two previously autonomous companies; this was to be the beginning of a new journey together. Both the purpose of the challenge and the desired outcome (in a very specific timeframe) had to be understood.

One particular member of the senior management team was falling about the room, and people were shouting at each other in frustration. The president's immediate action was to call for factory workers from their local manufacturing site, as he believed they would hopefully be younger and therefore more capable of standing up from a cross-legged position several times simultaneously.

Achievements do not always need to be clearly planned with all the known risks managed. There was little preparation for this event, and nobody had successfully completed the task prior to the event. All they had was the vision of success.

> "Achievements do not always need to be clearly planned with all the known risks managed."

Whilst the factory workers were brought together, the original team was starting to find a winning approach, beginning with the required circle of people linking arms and facing outwards. During the various trial and error attempts, individuals were starting to be recognized for their individual skills, and they began taking the lead to complete tasks. For example, the leader of the company's Indian business was able to stand easily from a cross-legged position. As there were many in the group who simply could not do this, he moved a number of people to one side of the room and started to teach them his technique. Nobody had asked him to do this; he just did it.

Shift 4: Engaging the players

It soon became clear that the original team that had begun the challenge did not have the capabilities required to achieve the goal, and a "new game"' had to be devised.

People quickly looked for alternative solutions outside of the immediate environment.

As the president had suggested, factory floor workers were sent invitations to join. It was hoped that these people would be younger and possibly more suited to the task.

A natural filtering process began to evolve. Those that were not capable of standing up from cross-legged joined together as a group, and requested they be placed at intervals in the circle. That way, those more capable would help them to stand, and then everybody could take part. This approach was tested, but the circle of people still kept collapsing.

The decision was taken that not all the team could take part in the exercise, so other important roles were created.

Those who were not taking part in the exercise started to act as marshals and encouragers, positioned at points around the circle, what was beginning to become a larger, more capable circle of people attempting the goal.

There was no proven path, formal hierarchy or procedure to achieving this world record, which gave space for people to come forward purely based on abilities and leadership skills specific to the challenge. So a new team was formed, and it became established and mobilized very quickly. In this new game, every runner had the chance to win a medal!

Shift 5: Cutting through the DNA

The new game had a very clear purpose, and when it is so clear, things get done – regardless of the nationality and background of the people involved.

The existing DNA was broken quickly.

The clarity of purpose cut through both the cultural and organizational DNA. Perceptions about the different cultures and the language barriers started to fall away, until the formal hierarchies had been dissolved.

The Japanese participants had no training, no planning, no detailed procedures and very little time to practice. This was something alien to their culture, but they took part without question, immersed themselves in the challenge to achieve our goal.

At this point some of the management team was losing confidence. Commentators were starting to become a powerful influence. "This is ridiculous; we have no hope of succeeding." "It was a childish idea and a waste of time." "How much did all this cost anyway?"

Another problem arose. We now didn't have enough team members capable of breaking the record, but we continued practising until the factory workers arrived, greeted by one of our Latin American team. He was so pleased to see them that his arms were waving in the air, and he was shouting with excitement.

Shift 6: Keeping the organization future-focused

Conversations had to move quickly from concerns about how this goal could be achieved to a clear focus on finding a solution and the new skills needed.

For the first half hour, the conversation was about 70% commentary.

During the second half hour there was chaos, as action-orientated conversations about what was missing began to compete with each other. But all the while the clear deadline began to create alignment – and in the last hour the conversations and actions became very focused on the outcome.

A selection process was introduced, and the Japanese factory workers were tested to see if they could stand from cross-legged. If they could they were recruited, but if not they had to stand aside. There was no time left for explanations. None of these new recruits spoke good English, so we had to explain by doing.

Shift 7: Gaining energy from setbacks

The big setback was that there still weren't enough people who were capable of standing up from a cross-legged position. This was just one of several setbacks, and they had to be used positively in some way to gain and maintain momentum.

In looking for what was missing, a process was identified. It was quickly decided that people would be given three chances. If after three tries they still couldn't manage it, they were asked to step aside. Some people chose to step outside and give up, but their commentary no longer had any power.

> "In looking for what was missing, a process was identified."

Others found another useful role, and they helped to achieve the goal in a different way.

We proceeded with a circle of 48 people, and with the help of the marshals we started to coordinate and improve our technique. The new Japanese recruits grasped the idea quickly.

With 15 minutes to go, we finally made what felt like a successful attempt. The energy could have blown the windows out! There was hope and renewed determination. The second attempt was even more successful. Due to time constraints, we had to be judged for our world record on only our third attempt. If we didn't make this, we would fail.

The room fell silent, awaiting a trigger to start from the judges. By now, some people had stood up nearly 40 times during practice, and legs were tired! The signal was given, we stood up together, and we could sense immediately that it was a success. People of all cultures, languages and positions within both organizations were jumping around the room in delight. The noise was overwhelming. Success felt great!

The power of emotion generated through successive attempts, failures and increasing progress was significant. The difference between success and failure was very small, and the final 15 minutes were highly emotional, playing a crucial role in our success. Once we had shown our ability to complete one stand-up (albeit a clumsy one), the rest was history. The team now believed success was possible, whereas previously it had been considered an impossible task or simply a pipedream.

Going forward, this world record achievement proved to be a powerful example of how people can work together, regardless of culture, language and specialism. A brand new context was created for the following two days of the conference, and the world record became a symbol signaling the start of a new era for this global organization.

FINAL THOUGHTS

The demand for us to write this book came from the people we work with, who asked us to capture the essence of what we do.

There are many ways to create transformations, and transformation can be achieved at many different levels. The approach we outline in this book, using the Magnificent Seven Shifts, has been proven during 20 years of working with people and organizations all over the world. It has proved successful at both an individual and organizational level, and is often found to be a life-changing experience for people at a very personal level.

It's fun! Transformation is a creative journey, where you continually adapt and carve your way through unchartered territory.

It's not for the faint-hearted! It can be scary, and you need a willingness to be uncomfortable as you will be testing approaches and resolving setbacks publicly. The very essence of this is captured beautifully in Nelson Mandela's inaugural address, 1995:

> *"Our worst fear is not that we are inadequate. Our deepest fear is that we are powerful beyond measure. It is our light, not our darkness, that most frightens us.*

We ask ourselves, 'Who am I to be brilliant, gorgeous, talented and fabulous?' Actually, who are you not to be?

You are a child of God; your playing small doesn't serve the world. There is nothing enlightened about shrinking so that other people won't feel insecure around you.

We were born to make manifest the glory of God within us, it is in everyone and as we let our own light shine, we unconsciously give other people permission to do the same.

As we are liberated from our own fear, our presence automatically liberates others."

The Magnificent Seven approach is a teachable and repeatable set of skills and processes. All you need to succeed are the will, the belief and the desire to achieve extraordinary results.

We hope that we have ignited your interest in this approach to transformation. We are establishing an organization committed to developing leaders who can make extraordinary things happen by design, and if you would like to find out more, please contact us:

Paul Adams – paul.adams@extraordinarypeople.co.uk

Mike Straw – mike.straw@extraordinarypeople.co.uk

ABOUT THE AUTHORS

Paul Adams

Paul has a wealth of knowledge from senior executive roles in the industrial, healthcare, consumer products and retail sectors. Paul's experience covers both Private Equity and Plc ownership together with leadership roles developing business and operations across Europe, Americas and Asia.

Over the past 20 years Paul has contributed significantly to the success of leading FTSE 100 brands such as Diageo plc, The Co-operative Group and Smith & Nephew plc. Then leading in the success of Talaris Ltd, and recently Glory Global Solutions Ltd as CEO.

Mike Straw

Mike's passion in business is people, specifically how organizations and the people within them can truly thrive and achieve things that they could only have dreamed of being possible. He has been designing and delivering award-winning change and transformation programmes for many local and global organizations since 1993 when he joined Breakthrough Technologies.

He founded Achieve Breakthrough in 2003 and works closely with his clients, delivering bespoke Breakthrough Thinking and Performance Programmes enabling them to liberate, achieve and sustain significant step changes and business performance improvements.

Mike is an International speaker and author. His earlier career was in operations, where he saw the limits that people were putting on themselves in relation to what was possible which, as a result, created the impetus to set up Achieve Breakthrough. This has now won consultancy of the year twice in the last three years – extraordinary!

The organizations that draw upon Mike and his colleagues range from leading pharmaceuticals, to high-tech companies and entrepreneurial organizations.

ACKNOWLEDGEMENTS

From Paul:

To those who, over the years, helped bring this book to life, and to those close to me who put up with the disruption over the past years caused by my determination to succeed.

From Mike:

In addition to the amazing companies we have worked with over the years, I want to thank all the transformation specialists that we have learned from and worked with: In particular Tracy Goss, Jim Selman, Geoffrey Higgins, Peter Sheahan, Fritjof Capra, Ray Anderson, Peter Senge and finally Emily Wright and Tara Burton for their drive and support in the creation of this book.

THE EXTRAORDINARY PEOPLE CLUB ...

The messages and learning in this book may appear simple. However, not easy to introduce as actually creating and living the required shifts in mindset and behaviour, along with building the muscles to make extraordinary things happen, is very challenging. So we believe it would be easier if you had some help. You can now take advantage of the extraordinary people club. Think of the club as a coming together of like-minded people who look to further develop themselves, strive for extraordinary change and have the real determination to make things happen.

There are meetings arranged during the year and a supporting series of learning tools and initiatives that are designed to further embed the concepts in this book – if you want to sign up for the extraordinary people club and training and development opportunities please email hello@extraordinarypeople.co.uk.

"An **extraordinary** person is someone who consistently does the things ordinary people can't do or won't do."

Nido R. Qubein, President,
High Point Universty